Flotsam and Jetsam

The Cranse Chronicles

About the author

BOB ROSS BEGAN sailing at the age of ten in the P-class trainer at the Plimmerton Boating Club on the shores of Cook Strait, New Zealand; he progressed to the two-handed Z-class then three-handed Idle Along.

After working in Wellington and New Plymouth as a journalist, Ross moved to Australia in 1955, aged 24 and worked on newspapers as a general reporter: Launceston Examiner (Tasmania), Daily Telegraph (Sydney) and finally the Sun News-Pictorial (Melbourne) from 1959.

At the Sun-Pic, in his spare time, he started a general boating column and began covering sailing. He went sailing again, on 21ft restricted class open boats, Lightweight Sharpies, Finns and keelboats on Port Phillip Bay and offshore.

Through Finns he met Colin Ryrie, the 1964 Olympic representative and 1964-65 Australian Finn class champion, who recruited him to be first editor of Modern Boating magazine, founded by Ryrie and business partner Jules Feldman, as the next magazine to Modern Motor in their growing Modern Magazines chain in Sydney.

After six years, Ross resigned and went freelance to become yachting correspondent for the Sydney Morning Herald and to write books.

With Ken McLachlan, business partner and advertising manager, he founded Australian Sailing, Australia's first all-sailing magazine, in 1976. He sold the magazine to the Yaffa Publishing Group of leisure magazines in 1986, remained as editor until 2003 and has since continued to contribute feature articles and Bob Cranse's By the Way column to the magazine.

Flotsam and Jetsam

The Cranse Chronicles

By Bob Cranse

(and his alter ego Bob Ross)

First published in 2016
Copyright 1976-2011 © Bob Ross
All rights reserved.

Published by Boatswain Books • www.boatswainbooks.uk

ISBN: 978-1-912724-11-6

Designed and produced by Robert Deaves

All rights reserved. No part of this publication may be reproduced by any means, electronic or mechanical, including photocopy or any information retrieval system without the prior written permission of the copyright owner.

CONTENTS

FOREWORD	by Sir James Hardy	7
PREFACE	Bob Cranse	9
CHAPTER 1	1976 to 1986	11
CHAPTER 2	1986 to 1996	61
CHAPTER 3	1996 to 2011	101

Foreword

IT HAS BEEN my pleasure to have known Bob Ross since the 1960s and during my ocean racing years, he was one of my regular crewmen.

Bob was very competent, diligent and reliable. He also was never sea sick!

In the early days I remember he wrote articles for the late Colin Ryrie in Colin's new magazine Modern Boating and in addition also became the much respected yachting writer for the Sydney Morning Herald for many years.

When Bob founded his own monthly magazine Australian Sailing in 1976 he introduced a contributing journalist, Bob Cranse, who wrote very interesting and amusing stories in his column each edition, 'Scuttlebutt'.

Few people were aware that Bob Cranse was actually a nom de plume of Bob Ross, the founder and editor of his magazine.

It was a very clever scheme, because Ross could continue to maintain his always accurate detail, whether in editorial comment, yacht racing activities, reports on new boats or other maritime developments whereas Bob Cranse was able to write whatever he liked without diminishing the accuracy or integrity of the Australian Sailing magazine.

I think it is a wonderful concept to group some of these famous Bob Cranse stories into one publication and I'm sure it will adorn the bookshelves of all those who relate to John Masefield's lovely poem Sea Fever:

I must go down to the seas again, to the lonely sea and the sky,
And all I ask is a tall ship and a star to steer her by;
And the wheel's kick and the wind's song and the white sail's shaking, And a grey mist on the sea's face, and a grey dawn breaking.

I must go down to the seas again, for the call of the running tide
Is a wild call and a clear call that may not be denied;
And all I ask is a windy day with the white clouds flying,
And the flung spray and the blown spume, and the seagulls crying.

I must go down to the seas again, to the vagrant gypsy life,
To the gull's way and the whale's way where the wind's like a whetted knife;
And all I ask is a merry yarn from a laughing fellow-rover,
And quiet sleep and a sweet dream when the long trick's over.

Sir James (Jim) Hardy O.B.E
Sydney, July 2016

Bob Cranse

LEGENDARY Sydney Sun yachting writer Lou d'Alpuget created Bob Cranse when he asked Bob Ross to write his regular column while he was overseas.

Ross was at the time yachting correspondent for the Sydney Morning Herald (those were the days when the sports sections of the dailies consistently covered yachting), so had to use a nom de plume to file for another paper.

But which one? Not long before, they had been in conversation watching the re-launching ceremony for the Hardy family's veteran gaff cutter Nerida at the Royal Sydney Yacht Squadron.

D'Alpuget owned another traditional yacht, the raised-decker Josephine designed by Cliff Gale. The Gale family was outraged when d'Alpuget replaced the original keel with a more modern version designed by Ben Lexcen.

So Cliff's son Roger, no fan of d'Alpuget's, sidled up to d'Alpuget and Ross at the Nerida re-launch with a question to test their nautical knowledge credentials and to score a point over d'Alpuget. "What's a cransine?" he snapped and rapidly moved away, leaving them puzzled.

The following week d'Alpuget rang Ross, excitedly. "I've got it!" he said. "Roger meant cranse iron, the fitting that caps the end of a bowsprit or bumpkin."

So d'Alpuget, recognising Ross as a bit of a country bumpkin, suggested Bob Cranse as the by-line for the fill-in yachting columnist for the Sun.

When Ross co-founded Australian Sailing magazine and decided to introduce an off-beat column he again needed another name, with his own on the editor's column only a few pages away, to spread the impression the magazine had a big editorial staff, instead of just him.

This item in an early column set the tone for much of what followed and revealed where Cranse collected most of his material:

Stern light
It's amazing what you can pick up at yacht club bars besides poundage around the waistline. As well as good advice on everything to do with boats, women and dogs, there is the occasional anecdote that is printable. "And so," says the ocean racing refugee now in the Soling class, "we are chasing the

stern light of this other yacht up the coast. Knowing the boat ahead is well navigated, the rest of the watch retires below out of the cold to enjoy a cuppa leaving the captain at the helm.

"What we don't know is the other boat turns off its navigation lights and tacks out to sea. Our skipper calls down: 'We're catching him; his stern light is much bigger.' I take a look and in the stern light can see a lady washing the dishes. So we crash tack and just miss the rocks under the kitchen window."

THE COLUMN GAINED momentum over the next ten years and Ross also included humour in some of the magazine's feature articles, a few of which are included here to provide snoozing-off opportunities through the staccato-attack items from *By the Way*.

1976 to 1986

Windsurfers do it standing up
WINDSURFING IS OBVIOUSLY a marvellous new compartment of the sailing sport. It calls for fitness and an agility of limb and mind. Hughie Treharne, sailmaker and ocean racing heavy, was zapping around Middle Harbour, I suppose more or less under control, when a speedboat pinned him inside a pier.

Windsurfers for some reason have no brakes; Hughie was heading at speed for the pier, which loomed as a distinct threat to his kneecaps. Thinking quickly, he picked up the mast and sail kit and caboodle, hopped up onto the pier, strolled across and rejoined his board as it slid out the other side. Wonder what it is that windsurfers do standing up!

Cudmore's cannon
HAROLD CUDMORE, THE Irishman who sailed Silver Shamrock to second place in the Half Ton Cup world championship sailed from Sydney in December 1977, is a whimsical chap.

He and some accomplices relocated an ornamental brass cannon from near the front door at the Royal Sydney Yacht Squadron to the winner's table at the presentation dinner. Well, what else would you plant on the table of a boat called Gunboat Rangiriri?

Oh yes, they filled it with brandy and spent the rest of the evening either trying to drink the contents or light it. There was a feeling after the event that the august old club will never be quite the same.

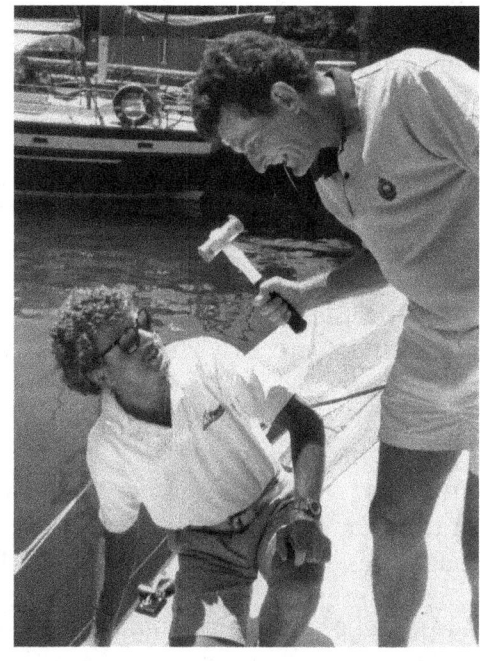

Harold Cudmore gives Geoff Stagg of Farr Yacht Design some friendly advice on construction

Taking on ballast

I WAS DISCUSSING the case of the 18-footer for'ard hand who dived overboard after a disagreement with his skipper with Ken Beashel. And Beasho, as usual, came up with one about as good, if not better:

Years ago he was sailing as a bailer boy on an 18, struggling along in a big breeze, when they came upon a competitor capsized and in those grand old days when buoyancy was considered to be sissy, hopelessly swamped.

The skipper eyed the bodies in the water and hissed to the biggest one: "Want a ride in?" They picked up the heavyweight and with his help sailed stiff as a church to the finish, no questions asked.

Sayonara was not goodbye

"SAD FAREWELL TO the Sayonara Cup", the headline jumped out of the Financial Review. The report went on to relate that the famous old interstate challenge trophy had been sold at auction for "a song, a mere $320", to Barton's Antiques in Sydney and there followed a well-researched history of the cup, awarded in 1904 by Alfred Gollin of Melbourne who won it himself in Sayonara.

With the glee of someone onto something BIG, the reporter added: "The trophy was catalogued merely as a 'large two-handled trophy cup' with no hint of the great Australian yachting challenges for which it was presented."

The item set off a string of minor explosions in the board rooms and yacht clubs of Melbourne, where they have a strong sense of tradition that soon steadied into a heavy barrage of flak directed towards the Royal Sydney Yacht Squadron.

A strangled 'phone call from a flag officer to the club took the creases out of the house manager's pin-stripe pants and had the secretary sprinting around to the trophy cabinet. There, where it has reposed since Bill Northam won it for the Squadron with Saskia, sat the Sayonara Cup, undisturbed.

The club and the antique dealer quickly communicated and it seems the trophy sold at auction was a replica, a very faithful replica that even repeats a misspelling in the engraving. It was made probably for Gollin to keep. Meantime the reporter retired to bed with the 'flu.

Chas from Tas appears

THE FIRST OF many references to Charles (Chas from Tas) Blundell appeared in the Cranse column in April 1978. It identified him as the brother of the magazine's Tasmanian correspondent Richard Blundell and went on...

Wild of eye and manner, Chas has been a paid hand on North American yachts for the last few years. I saw him in Cowes last year, making his way gingerly down the street to join a Brazilian Admiral's Cup team yacht, Tigre, with 20 minutes to go to the start.

Well Chas has won the Rio Circuit regatta in the most unusual circumstances. His owners could not afford the time off to sail the last and deciding race, a 180-miler, so let Chas skipper their S&S 40 called Peanut Brittle.

Incredibly, the skippers of the other boats conferred on the starting line, decided to sail a shortened course, told each other but no-one thought to tell Chas and there were no official course-shortening signals.

So Chas went off and sailed the full course, finishing just as the prizes were to be presented. "Either Chas has made the biggest navigational cock-up of his life or perhaps he has actually sailed the whole course," said his owner at the presentation." That remark dropped a heavy silence over the gathering that deepened as they saw the protest flag hoisted in the rigging of Peanut Brittle.

Chas from Tas (right) with Hong Kong friend and yacht owner Dr Ian Nicholson

The protest was accepted, all the other boats were listed as "did not finish" and so Peanut Brittle became the 1977 winner of the Rio Circuit. "All the trophies had to be re-listed to be presented in ten minutes' time as we had arrived just as the first prize was being presented and the big spread was about to be eaten," reported Chas in a letter home to Richard.

"I felt very bad about it but every navigator and 90 per cent of the skippers applauded the incident as the best thing that has happened in the ocean racing scene here in years."

Benny and the jets

Bob Ross in early 1977 visited Yanchep, north of Perth to watch some of the trials between the new Ben Lexcen/Johan Valentijn America's Cup challenger Australia and Alan Bond's 1974 challenger Southern Cross, which was designed by Lexcen (at that time Bob Miller before he changed his name). He recorded:

AUSTRALIA HAS A tiny hull, big rig, is lively in the lightest winds, manoeuvrable, accelerates quickly, stable in a moderate-fresh breeze and has a very low pitching moment. Over the two days racing I watched the new yacht win

Ben Lexcen (right) and Ron Packer share a laugh on the eventful sail with Benny and the Jets off Yanchep in 1977

every start and every race against Southern Cross.

The whole operation at Yanchep is much more open-handed and relaxed than in 1974 when I hid in the bushes and aboard a crayfishing boat to watch Southern Cross' early sailing and had furtive meetings in the evenings with Bob Miller.

Access this time is unlimited and Bob, now Ben, even invites me aboard Southern Cross for the day's sailing against Australia: "Come with us, we've only got 13 today."

The crew on the warm-up boat calls itself "Benny and the Jets" after the Elton John hit of the time. "The Jets" are mostly youngsters eager to learn, sights set on the next challenge or gathering experience for big-yacht ocean racing. With as many as five them at times fighting to do the same job, sailing with them is entertaining.

Benny is calmer than the old Bob Miller. He's had a health scare … high blood pressure … but is getting over that with medication, and a much more relaxed outlook on life (well that's what I think before the racing starts).

And he is really sailing this boat well. The mainsail leech looks shot with stretch distortion but the general shape is not bad. A re-cut six ounce headsail looks good and is proving to be an effective sail through a wide range and he had added inner sheeting tracks which have improved Southern Cross' light air performance.

Australia is going faster today with more mast bend, thanks to the removal of the jumpers. She catches us port and starboard on the line in one start through her smaller turning circle and slow trim by The Jets but we sail on and gain the lead when Australia's crew fouls a sheet through grinding a loose spinnaker sheet through the genoa block and has to tack away to clear it.

Australia rolls us over quite easily in the second race, really fast to windward in 10 to 12 knots. Then her crew has problems with the twin-grooved headfoil while trying to change genoas as the wind increases over 15 and loses to us.

Now it's The Jets' turn for drama. We have to change to a heavier headsail too. A wave picks up the old sail as it is being unhanked and washes it overboard, taking one of The Jets with it. We pick him up and in the process another Jet goes over the side.

Then Benny is displeased with The Jet manning the spinnaker pole topping lift. "If you don't get your head up out of that hatch and have a look next time you have to lift that pole, I'll come up there and knock it off your shoulders," he says, sounding just like the old Bob Miller. We return to the harbour for lunch.

There are no fancy tenders in this no-frills campaign. The boats sail in and out of the very narrow entrance and dock. A launch with only one of its two engines working is ready to tow them out again.

We race once more. This time we start ahead and to leeward in about eight knots. Within 400 yards Australia sails straight over the top of us. We throw a few tacks, they cover and keep going away, vastly superior.

Benny mutters: "I'm not really aggressive today; I've taken too many blood pressure pills." The Jet manning the topping lift might not agree.

We cannot make any impression on Australia, even though we cheat and bear away 200 yards short of the windward mark. Then Benny tries to put The Jets through a spinnaker gybe/set that ends in a gigantic mess.

The problem is not helped by Benny and Ron Packer, the navigator/tactician, yelling conflicting instructions at the foredeck and then yelling at each other in something that sounds like a passage from Grand Opera as each realises the other has different views on how it should be done.

With Australia long gone, The Jets try again, step by step, and again there's a mess-up with the brace catching in a jib hank and two now thoroughly stirred up Jets fighting on the point for the privilege of releasing it.

Benny soon cools it down, starts a long and funny monologue about his experiences with the telephone system in Italy and with the breeze dropping right out, both boats return to the marina.

Kevin Shephard, pun master

A FEW YEARS have passed since I sailed a Hobart race with Kevin Shephard whose jokes were ruled to be so rancid he was allowed only five minutes each hour to tell them. His "It's too loose Lautrec" for slack jib luff or mainsail foot tension is one of his better funnies so you can see how desperate things became.

The man does not improve with age. I have just returned from a Sydney-Brisbane race with Sheppo, riddled in mind and body by bad puns. Our Czechoslovakian-born caterer George Mottle, who managed to produce European-style cuisine from a shoebox someone with a sense of humour christened a galley aboard John Biddlecombe's Casablanca, became untypically angry one day when someone complained that 28 of the 30 sandwiches were salami. "Crossed Czech", explained Sheppo.

Bad puns aside, he did leave me pondering a winning philosophy for race losers: "Only but for if we would have."

Ronnie Biggs, Fireball sailor!

At the 1978 PanAm Clipper Cup in Hawaii, Charles Blundell (Chas from Tas) whose exploits on behalf of Brazilian yacht owners have been mentioned in this column before, told me that Ronald Biggs, the Great Train Robber, who has found a reasonably pleasant-looking sanctuary in Brazil, was building himself a Fireball using the carpentry skills he learned in jail.

Ronnie also told Charles that he enjoyed his stay in Australia because Australians had a special affection for crims and wouldn't mind living here if we could get rid of the flies. Here's a chance for the Australian Fireball Association to import a real fund raiser!

Don't forget

As I am so forgetful myself, I love stories about people who forget things. I suppose almost everybody has at some time turned up for a race without buoyancy vest, rudder, vital sail, etc.

One of my old Finn sailing friends Ken Murrell starred in my favourite story of this type. Ken, who lives at Seaforth, was racing keenly in the Finn fleet that those days sailed on Botany Bay. He arrived at the Bay one Saturday only to find he had left his rudder behind. So he drove like a maniac back home, retrieved the rudder and was suddenly aware of distressing noises being made by his pregnant wife.

"Oh alright," he muttered. "I'll drop you off at the maternity hospital on the way. But hurry up or I'll miss the start. Ken made the start, became a father and believe it or not, remained married to the same charming lady.

Incredibly the other day I lobbed onto a forgetful story even better than that one. The hero is a very high-powered mover in skiffs with a reputation for total un-recall.

There he was, packing up after a 16ft skiff carnival in Brisbane, intent that nothing, just nothing, should be left behind. Sail bags, rudder, tiller, masts, booms, poles were individually checked off as they were packed carefully for the trip home to Sydney. It was not until he was driving into Surfers Paradise that the blinding flash struck him down – he had forgotten to hook the boat and trailer onto the car.

From Harold Cudmore
HAROLD CUDMORE, THE renowned Irish sailor who is never lost for words, after breaking two masts on Quarter Apple during the 1978 Quarter Ton Cup world championship in Japan, observed: "This is a variation on the Biblical story of the apple falling out of the tree... this time, the tree kept falling out of the Apple."

Sharing the steering
WHAT DO YOU do with yourself while struggling the boring miles home after pulling out of an ocean race, except perhaps sticking pins into an effigy of the skipper or trying to find the hiding place for the rum.

Well you can organise little competitions, as did the crew of Casablanca dragging their tails homeward from a non-finish in the 1978 Montagu Island race.

It started, I think, with the remark about renowned Araldited-on helm

All hands to the wheel, with Kevin Shephard calling the shots on the way home after retirement from the 1978 Montagu Island race

holders: "When I heard Sheppo and Lawso were on the same watch, I thought the boat must have two steering wheels!"

A debate began on the pros and cons of giving everyone a steer and having a say in which way to go led to the big experiment. The whole crew of ten, except the stooge holding the camera, packed the helmsman's cockpit and got a hand to the wheel. Is this a record?

Sheppo solutions

THE EDITOR IS back from Melbourne with not much to show in the way of results for sailing on Jim Hardy's Nyamba in the 1979 Admiral's Cup trials but with a sort of a sun tan that mostly hides his ghastly pallor and some fodder for this column.

He had the fortune (?) to sail once more with Kevin Shephard, fine-touch helmsman and stand-up comic. Said Hardy on a calm day: "I wish we could heel the yacht over a little bit more."

Said Shephard: "Well you could take a halyard out to the windward rail and winch it up."

After the third day of sailing, when it became obvious that the altered Nyamba was probably not fast enough to be selected in the Australian team, Hardy said: "Well we may not make it but I will save myself $10,000 by not going to England.

Shephard commented: "Give the crew $5000 now and we'll make sure of it for you. You'll still be $5000 in front.

One of the heavies on Marloo did a bundle on the trials, but not by betting on the outcome. He was sitting across the tail of a runner that was so enthusiastically trimmed back and forth that it cut through the hip pocket of his jeans and $70 drifted away on Port Phillip Bay.

Man in the Iron Mask

OVER THE YEARS I have enjoyed many variations of the "Man in the Iron Mask" theme joke played on people who drink too much and pass out. A famous Australian yachting journalist, as an ordinary journalist in a previous life, held a party in his hotel room when he was on an away assignment in Melbourne.

His mates (?) locked him in a wardrobe, carried it downstairs and left it in the lobby in the early hours of the morning.

And I have long memories myself of seeing Sticky Armitage, the Kiwi now on lend-lease to the yanks, asleep under a table at a cocktail party the Australians gave in a Plymouth hotel one Admiral's Cup. They surrounded him with a fence of champagne bottles, turned out the lights and left him there.

And there was the time that Bob Fisher, the cheery Pom yachting writer, fell asleep while clutching a can of beer aboard Ragamuffin after a Hobart race. So that he wouldn't drop the can, some kind soul got out the silicone gun and wrapped an immovable bond around his hands and the can.

Well the latest of this type of story in my collection is the one about the crewman on a Half Tonner in this season's very slow Hobart race (1978) who had foolishly committed himself to a ride on another boat in the Great Circle race (810n miles starting from Portsea, Victoria, around Tasmania clockwise and return to finish at Flinders) as an encore. But by the time he reached Hobart, he was fed up with ocean racing, swore he would never go again, told the skipper of the yacht he was to go on when he came around that night that he was a definite non-starter.

What with the fatigue and a couple of Cascades, he was soon sleeping peacefully. His mates packed up his gear, carried it and him over to the Melbourne-bound Great Circle entry. He obligingly stayed asleep next morning through the racket of getting under way and went back towards Bass Strait without even setting foot on the dock.

The skipper of the Half Tonner presumes he enjoyed the Great Circle – but he has never received a "thank you" call.

Elephant's trunk

AN INTERSTATE VISITOR to a class national championship in Sydney (no names, to avoid embarrassment, not to mention lawsuits) took his family to Bullen's Animals World on the lay day.

They ranged through the park viewing the wild animals and everything was going beautifully until one of the daughters accidentally pressed the button that wound down one of the power windows. An elephant standing alongside put his trunk through the window. The daughter panicked, hit the button again to wind up the window and jammed the poor elephant's trunk.

The elephant panicked and in struggling to get free broke the window and kicked in the side of the family car, which happened to be a Mercedes. This upset the visitor so much that he repaired nerves with a "liquid lunch" at the nearest pub.

On the way back to the championship venue they came across a road accident. The wife prevailed on her husband to stop so she could assist the injured with her nursing capabilities.

When the cops arrived, they immediately embraced the damaged Mercedes as part of the accident scene, wouldn't believe the husband's pleas of non-involvement, nor his story of the car door being kicked in by an elephant (well, would you?) and invited him to breathe into the bag. The result of all this was a fine and disqualification from driving for a month.

You will notice I have resisted the temptation of writing, "they pronounced him elephant's trunk."

'Raw Meat's' teeth shower

RUSSELL SLADE, ANNOUNCING the sponsorship by his company Bonds Coats Patons of an 18ft skiff to be called Chesty Bond, skippered by Trevor Barnabas, recalling his own days skippering 18s, said he was sailing with George ("Raw Meat") Pearce on the sheet and badly wanted to gybe. The mainsheet was tangled and George had the end between his teeth as he tried to sort it out.

Sladey could wait no longer, crash-gybed the boat and was horrified to see teeth showering into the bilge. But no blood emerged from George; just a strongly-worded lament for a smashed denture.

Champion's luck

DON BUCKLEY THE forward hand celebrated so conscientiously after Iain Murray's Color 7 sewed up the 1979 JJ Giltinan international 18-footer championship with one heat to sail that he forgot to put the three spinnakers on for the remaining heat the following day.

When Murray called for a spinnaker at the first mark, Buckley rummaged around and discovered instead the awful truth. All they had in the boat was a flat-cut reaching spinnaker sometimes hoisted in hurricanes.

They had the series won anyway so just laughed, more or less, at Don's embarrassment and sailed on, down the first reach, with the pocket-handkerchief reacher.

Then blow me down, the wind came ahead and started to freshen. The opposition under their big kites began to tumble over and in the end Murray,

Iain Murray, Don Buckley and Andrew Buckland with the JJ Giltinan Trophy

Buckley and Andrew Buckland won that heat as well. As they say, champions make their own luck.

Bumblebee 4's dismasting

IT IS NOT true, as someone suggested afterwards, that John Kahlbetzer, Bumblebee 4's owner observed after the mast of his brand new maxi sloop went over the side, "It was like driving a Rolls Royce off the foredeck."

John, remarkably cool and philosophical about the disaster, merely observed: "Well that takes care of crew training tomorrow."

Seasickly insane

THE SUBJECT WAS seasickness and after everyone in the group made some kind of revolting contribution of experiences with chronic sufferers, Harold Vaughan got the gong and ended the discussion with this one:

He was skippering a yacht hammering along the coast in a rough Bird Island race. A new crew member, whose bank balance was obviously bigger than his bank of sailing experience, was lying in the cockpit, miserably seasick.

They took a dig into Cape Three Points and the sufferer, catching sight of land, offered Harold a large sum of money to buy the life raft so he could go ashore. Harold passed up the opportunity of a lifetime and declined.

Then the sufferer began taking off his shoes and socks, determined to swim for it. Harold had to put about and take a leg out to sea while a couple of crewmen held the demented one down.

Clem under-caters

I NEVER CEASE to be amazed by the wisdom that pours – along with other things – from our older and more experienced ocean-racing sailors. I mean, what would you do if you invited a team of people home for a meal and found there were not enough steaks to feed them all. For most people, a sprint to the nearest Chinese takeaway would solve the problem. But on the ocean, there is a remarkable absence of fast-food outlets (next opening for McDonalds?).

This sort of problem faced my friend Clem Masters, who has been up and down and round and round on the Australian coast for 100 years, when he found he had under-catered by two steaks for a crew of nine on a recent race.

Clem never turned hair, which is just as well as he hasn't all that many to turn. He just asked in a general sort of way in the hearing of the two youngest and hungriest crew-members, "Who likes sausages?"

They snapped onto that one like a pair of terriers: "We like sausages, we like sausages."

"Good," said Clem. "You two can have sausages and the rest of us will have steak."

All bets are off

FOR YEARS I have gone along with officials and participants with the same blind faith that I have in Santa Claus, that betting no longer goes on in Sydney 18-footer sailing.

Ask about it and you would be told something like, "Oh just a few of the boys having a friendly bet among themselves." And perhaps that fellow muttering "five-to-four KB" on the ferry was really just ordering a few more tinnies.

The police apparently shared that view until a bunch of them in plain clothes, one with a flowing beard, ended a fine Sunday on the harbour recently by arresting 10 men on the two spectator ferries for betting.

It all happened politely and unobtrusively as the ferries tied up and people shuffled off – not a patch on the old days when bookies and punters jumped off the side of the ferry as the coppers clambered aboard the other, hid in the stokehold and the famous "Dick the Diver" earned his nickname by swimming ashore with the betting slips in his mouth.

One way or another, betting on the 18s has been going on since the class began in the 1900s. It was quite a "heavy" scene for a time. About 30 years ago a gun was pulled on a skipper rigging at Birchgrove with some friendly advice, like: "Run dead or else."

One well-known skipper worked a system of signals with punting friends on the ferry. If his handicap was right, the price was right and he felt confident of winning, he wouldn't wear his cap at the start. The cap would stay on if he was going to run dead.

Once, when this character looked in a good position after a strong run before a southerly towards the Sow and Pigs, he amazed a wide-eyed young crewman known to me with: "Okay, our handicap's not right, break something." With a bigger handicap the following week, he was a sure winner and the price was better.

The late and great Alf Beashel, for many years race secretary to the NSW 18ft Sailing Club, hated the betting but accepted it was part of the sport. When Alf was skippering his own 18, a bookmaker approached him in Double Bay park before a race and offered him 300 pounds to pull a race. Alf just said quietly, "Ask the crew."

The bookie did. Their reply was wordless. They just picked him and threw him into the bay.

Sydney-Hobart '79

THE 1979 SYDNEY-HOBART race was a relatively quiet one with the best stories coming from the party afterwards that about matches the race each year for elapsed time and endurance requirements.

But our editor told me a good one from the Clem Masters sailing school aboard Nyamba.

... Young crewman, after a flow of other pesky questions: "How fast do you think we are going?"

Clem: "Sixteen knots."

YC: "Yeah!"

Clem: "Eight knots down one side of the boat and eight down the other."

The Quiet Little Drink, that gathering of crewmen where songs are sung, stories told, beer inhaled, celebrated the end of its first decade by smashing the record with 11,105 beers poured. The previous best was 9450 in 1975.

Clem Masters, the fountain of wisdom for young sailors, at left with Sir James Hardy steering his Police Car in the 1981 Sydney-Hobart race and crewmen Neil Hoey and Malcolm Griffith

An amorphous mass (or mess) of 500 attended and raised $17,000 to go probably to a foundation for helping young Tasmanian ocean-racing yachtsmen gain overseas experience.

The southern hemisphere table-top tap-dancing championship ended in a tied decision between Sid Brown, Peter Bowker, Don Mickleborough and Bob Fisher.

The championship was different this year. Instead of the contestants going through the floor, they went through the roof. Standing on the tapping table, the bigger guys lacked headroom. Shifting some of the removable ceiling panel solved that problem and they tapped away with their heads in the ceiling. Anyone who has seen those heads can draw their own conclusions about the merit of that arrangement.

Fastnet storm survival

BEFORE HE WANDERED on to the next regatta in his life after the Southern Cross series in Sydney Peter Bowker, the most durable of all the paid hands on the international circuit, told me of his experiences in the 1979 Fastnet race when laughs were few (15 sailors lost their lives and 23 boats were abandoned).

He was navigating for Ted Turner on Tenacious. Ted keeps a dry ship but always has a couple of cases of canned beer hidden away somewhere on board for a small celebration after the race.

At the height of the storm Bowker was down below, trying to get some rest among the sail bags and like everyone else in the race at that time pondering his mis-spent past.

The storm trysail, about the last card in the pack, was called for. Bowker, who had been lying on it, passed it up. Beneath it, he found Turner's beer cache. So he had one. Well wouldn't you?

Key overboard

A South Australian yacht going home from the Sydney-Hobart race lost a man overboard. His rescue was considerably delayed when the crew found the swimmer had the key to the motor in his pocket.

Ambulance overlapped

Nicki Bethwaite on the way to Botany Bay to contest the Australian 470 championship had an argument with an ambulance. The ambulance, on its way to a simulated crash exercise at Kingsford Smith airport staged a disaster of its own. While trying to avoid another vehicle, it swerved into Nicki's trailer-borne 470 and damaged it substantially.

Nicki, one of those girls who never gives up, applied to the race committee for average points for heat one, which she missed while repairs were being made, under Rule 12 as a "yacht materially prejudiced".

The committee found against her but a note from its secretary Jim Orrell showed that race committees may have a streak of humanity after all:

"The Committee regrets that your application cannot be granted as Rule 12 only applies while a vessel is racing and if disabled by another vessel.

"The Committee has not considered whether the ambulance was the right-of-way vehicle or was trying to establish an overlap through and over your vehicle."

Finn ceremonial brick

I am reliably informed that the Finn class has a ceremonial brick, which it hands to newcomers. After they have bashed their heads against it 3000 times, they are deemed ready to take a Finn to windward in 20 knots on Botany Bay/Waterloo Bay/Port Phillip Bay.

The brick apart, the Finn attracts some amazing people. One of these is the former instructor of the Victorian Yachting Council's sail-training scheme Roy Hoffert who, at 60, decided he needed a fresh challenge.

He bought a Finn and entered the 1980 Olympic trials on Corio Bay. When a reporter from the Geelong Advertiser asked him about his physical preparation, pencil sharpened in anticipation of a flow on aerobics, anaerobics, glucose, nuts and brave pills, Roy replied: "I train on Corio whisky and peppermint. It keeps the body warm out on the water."

Bill Hooper's confidential index

ONE OF THE nicest things to happen to me on a visit to Melbourne for Sailboat '80 was the chance to sit around a cosy pot-bellied wood stove in the Jolly Roger boatshed at Albert Park Lake and have a yarn with Bill Hooper, who has the sailing school there.

The Hoopers have been on the lake for 100 years and Bill's son John and Buster, the successful 470 and Fireball combination, look like carrying on the family tradition through another generation.

Bill Hooper holds court at the Jolly Roger Boatshed on Albert Park, Melbourne, 1980

Bill has taught hundreds of people to sail, among them many who are well known today in sailing or business. Over the years he kept a card index on them all with frank comments on their progress and ability.

The index remained "strictly confidential" until recently when a now-famous ex-pupil begged for a look at his card. Reluctantly, Bill searched the system and produced the yellowing card.

It's concluding line was, "Last lesson not paid for."

Benny's America's Cup tray

IF BY SOME miracle Australia wins the America's Cup and by a miracle of equal magnitude they can actually prise it loose from the New York Yacht Club and out of the USA, all future racing is likely to be for the America's Tray.

Around 1970, when Alan Bond's yachting ambitions extended only to being a heavy in ocean racing, he took Apollo to America for the Newport-Bermuda race.

One of the American Twelve Metres was moored on the opposite side of the dock to Apollo and as any yachtsman would, Alan went over to have a "sticky beak".

In those days the Americans were paranoid about "industrial espionage" and tight security surrounded their America's Cup boats. So the crew boss of the Twelve popped out of the forehatch and gave Bondy a mouthful.

This so angered Apollo's designer Ben Lexcen, who happened to be on Apollo at the time, that he spouted back at the US heavy something sounding like:

Ben Lexcen with the America's Cup Plate, awarded during the 1983 America's Cup prizegiving

"I'll tell you what you can do with the America's Cup. We are going to come back here one day with a super yacht that will beat the pants off you.

"Then we are going to get your America's Cup and have a steam roller run over it again and again outside the New York Yacht Club."

Roll on the America's Cup Tray.

[The above story moved into America's Cup folklore so when Alan Bond's Lexcen-designed Australia II did win the Cup in 1983, the New York YC presented Lexcen with the Tray, a battered Chrysler hub cap.]

Underwater blooper

HERE'S ONE FOR the rules buffs, not to mention those who make winch handles and sails:

I ran into a trailer-sailer hot-shot (they are all more fanatical than the mum-and-dad image make them appear) who told me how he shocked and amazed the opposition by zooming past in no wind in a certain well-known night race.

With the fleet just drifting along on the current, he slipped his blooper over the side with a winch handle tied to each corner of the foot. The sail set beautifully under water in the current and gained him many places.

He asked whether I thought it was legal. Well now I am at a safe distance and have re-read Rule 60.1 (Means of Propulsion), I think he was cheating. The rule begins with: "A yacht shall be propelled only by the natural action of the wind on the sails, spars and hull, and water on the hull ... etc." But what a helluva'n idea.

World's worst pun

ALL THOSE WHO hate terrible puns should stop right here. Moving right along for the masochists ... we were in the middle, more or less, of Port Phillip Bay racing in near windless conditions, when the mid-deck mumblers began a deep discussion on cloud patterns left and right.

Two of them were well versed in the wind-behaviour research of Frank Bethwaite and began tossing around references to Frank's thoughts on matters like, "transverse roll systems", "air change onset", "Coriolis effect", "mature and cycling sea breeze" while trying to anticipate what, if anything the breeze would do next.

Someone asked an opinion from one whose wind research went a little deeper than the hot air second rank at the CYCA bar. Kevin Shephard said: "I think we had Betht waite and see."

Well I did warn you.

Tee-shirt messages

AFTER BORING EVERYONE to tears recently, tee shirt messages (I've even seen one reading "Admiral's Cup trials competitor". What next? "America's Cup runner-up") are improving.

On Lake Macquarie, the Cole 43 Polaris sliced into the Diamond Class Storm so deeply that Polaris' progress was halted only when the keel's leading edge came up hard against Storm's hull.

The following week, the Polaris crew arrived at Lake Macquarie Yacht Club with the boat's name on their shirts crossed out and replaced with "Diamond Cutter" (a successful One Tonner of that name races in Sydney).

And on the back was printed: "Royal Blind Sailing Club".

Hardy's hold on the wheel

MAINTENANCE WAS A never-ending task for America's Cup challenger Australia's crew at Newport, Rhode Island, in 1980. Everyone had a job including Jim Hardy who seemed to spend an awful lot of time working on Australia's steering.

US defender Freedom's tactician Dennis Durgan, intrigued by the sight of Hardy making yet another trip to the machine shop with the wheel under his arm, asked: "Why is Jim always carrying that wheel around?"

Explained Australia crewman John ("Steamer") Stanley: "He's dead frightened someone is going to take it from him!"

Message to the sailmaker

I'VE ONLY JUST caught up with the message to the sailmaker to end all such messages from David Kellett and the gang aboard Gretel after they dropped the stick and most of everything hanging onto it, over the side in the Montagu race.

They stuffed the remnants of the mainsail – only a strip of the foot left hanging on the boom – into the Hood repair bin at the Cruising Yacht Club of Australia with the note:

"Small tear 7ft above boom, please return by Wednesday."

Dis-chimneyed

DAVID KELLETT, WHO skippers Gretel for Bernard Lewis, is an out-going sort of chap. When the occasion arises at a party, he knows how to bring the house down.

The clash of Gretel with another Twelve converted to ocean racing, Nefertiti, was much to everyone's surprise as keen in this season's Sydney-Hobart as the advance publicity said it would be.

To celebrate Gretel's second overall placing, Kellett threw a party one afternoon at his home for his crew and that of Nefertiti. To provide shelter from the blazing sun, he rigged an old Twelve Metre spinnaker across the yard anchored to various points including the chimney of the house.

At some stage during the afternoon (the witnesses are understandably vague about times a details) a big gust of wind filled the spinnaker and the chimney sort of fell down.

Malcolm Fraser in Hardy's shoes

JIM HARDY IS taking special care of his new pair of Topsiders. Cast your mind back to the 1980 America's Cup and Prime Minister Malcolm Fraser's visit to Australia's crew.

Do you recall how the Prime Minister sailed Australia part of the way out to a start before dashing ashore to catch up with his official engagements?

Well, as the PM stepped aboard, Alan Bond was concerned that his street shoes might deposit him over the side. He made a quick check of shoe sizes and stopped at Hardy's 13EEs as the only ones big enough to fit Big Mal. "Let's have your shoes, Jim," hissed Bondy.

When the Prime Minister quit the boat to speed back to Newport in the Boston Whaler tender, he was still wearing Hardy's shoes. "Never mind," said Bond, "I will replace them," said Bond. And he has.

Hardy observes: "I couldn't hope to stand in the Prime Minister's shoes but it is nice to know he has stood in mine."

Mr Fraser enjoyed both the sail and the trip ashore. He was so impressed by the Boston Whaler that he subsequently bought one for his fishing trips. Could he be in the market for a Twelve Metre as well?

Animal's Cup trials

THE DOG JOKES started somewhere, sometime, back in Sydney between the crews of boats struggling to find form for the 1981 Admiral's Cup trials, to be held on Melbourne's Port Phillip Bay.

Based on the ancient premise that a slow boat is a dog, the thing quickly gathered momentum with suggestions that dog-catchers from various municipalities be called on to join the selection panel and that the event be named the RSPCA Cup.

Encouraging the dog at the 1981 Animal's Cup trials

To see the joke played out, I flew south on the Kerosene Canary, headed for the Sandringham Fishing and Fighting Club to shoot down a few Germaine Greers with me mates Frizzle, Doom, Groggo, Hanger, Zapper, etc and watch them try and sail that mighty heavy-weather machine Police Car in nil air or summink (this confusing vernacular is through spending too much time with Munno; from here it's straightened out).

Police Car had more than a modicum of locals on board whose advice comprised mainly the following, echoed over and over: "Jock always heads for the beach."

After following this sound meteorological assessment several times only to have the whole fleet pour by on shifts picked up towards the middle of the Bay, the general feeling grew on the Cop Car that Jock (Sturrock) headed for the beach in windless conditions only to catch a cab home.

The most popular expert call on board was, "We'll outsmart them this time," initiated on the approach to a gybe by Zapper, from the point, with the boat well positioned to drive over a rival and so secure second-last place.

In the event, the "outsmart'em' backfired when the lazy sheet threw itself around the end of the spinnaker pole and kept it pinned on the wrong side of the boat long enough to let the opposition off the leash.

The dog thing alleviated the lack of tension towards the back of the fleet where on every crossing there would be a lively chorus of dog howls. Packets of flea powder were transferred from one pan-licker to another; dog collars and cans of dog food appeared mysteriously overnight on pulpits.

Another variety of animal was represented at the trials – the noble horse. Ragamuffin had some sponsorship help from Tooths' Brewery (part of it in beer) and so carried crew shirts and battle flag with the brewer's horse's head emblem.

Well-wishers thoughtfully tied a bundle of hay over the boat's marina pen to keep it happy. There were suggestions that the hay could have been put to better use tied to the pulpit, encouraging Rags to break into a gallop during the racing.

Seasick cures

I WAS INTERESTED to read about the acupuncture method of preventing seasickness in the editor's column (moribund as usual), but only mildly so as I have a much better method: Drink a can of beer very slowly as you head out into open water.

I know many of you appreciate that I welcome ANY excuse to crack a tinny, but I'm serious; it works.

This cure was passed to me by Stanley Rosenfeld, the American yachting photographer, who inherited it from his father, one of the greatest yachting photographers of all times.

For the Rosenfelds, fighting off seasickness while trying to focus up on yachts from heavily rolling motor boats was a real hazard in marine photography.

If that fails, there is always Kevin Shephard's cure for seasickness: Sit under a tree for half an hour.

Curley's escapes

CURLEY IS ONE of those characters whose life seems to revolve completely around sailing and yachting clubs. You can find out his real name for yourself for reasons that will become apparent as you read on.

Next to sailing, Curley enjoys best having a drink and sometimes this leads him into bother, like the one in Sydney Harbour on a bitter winter's night.

Curley had dwelt over-long at a farewell party for the Ragamuffin crew before their departure for the 1981 Admiral's Cup at the Mosman Rowers – a friendly club in Mosman Bay that is the haunt of many north-side sailors. He missed his lift back across the Harbour Bridge to his home watering hole, the CYCA and looked around for an alternative means of transport.

Curley found an ancient canoe. It lacked paddles but Curley, who is not one to resist a challenge, began paddling it across the harbour with his hands.

Two-thirds of the way to the familiar lights of Darling Point, the old canoe gave up. Its seams opened, water poured in and Curley realised he was in bother once again.

He altered course for Clark Island; the canoe gurgled its last and he swam the remaining 300 metres to the island's shore. There is not a lot of traffic on the harbour at 2am and so Curley resigned himself to making the best of the rest of the night on the island.

The island in the past has been venue for shipwreck adventure plays, like

Treasure Island, that delight the kids. Curley somehow got a blazing fire going in a rubbish tin and began drying out. Just as warmth began restoring to his rapidly-sobering body, a heavy shower of rain doused the fire and Curley.

He spent the rest of the night alternately hiding under rock ledges and pacing the island to keep warm until rescue after dawn by two home-going Italian fishermen. "I just told them it was my buck's night and my mates had marooned me on the island," Curley explained. "They looked at me as though I was crazy."

Perceptive people, fishermen.

While Curley's escapade could have ended in tragedy, the bloke seems to have a charmed life. When I related it to some of his old friends in Hobson's Bay Yacht Club in Curley's home city Melbourne, one of them, "Dicko", almost topped it.

It seems Curley a few years ago fell from a Dragon while coming alongside the club's jetty. Dicko in trying to rescue Curley, who was wearing full waterproof gear and sea boots, fell on top of him.

Dicko climbed back aboard the Dragon and realised that only bubbles were coming up, no Curley. More bother. The water is shallow there and the bottom muddy. Dicko's fall had driven Curley into the mud and he was caught fast there, by his boots. The story, obviously, had a happy ending. Dicko got a handful of that tight curly hair and yanked Curley out of the mud and onto the surface.

Instant boat names
NAMING A BOAT is a task that has become even more tiresome with the insistence by race officials that a name must be displayed, of specified minimum size, on the hull.

Bruce Findlay of the Whitsunday Sailing Club, finding himself without a name for his Sonata 6.7 just before the start of the North Queensland JOG championship, raced out to a hardware shop to look for a ready-made name plate.

It was an easy choice from "Exit", "Ladies", "Gentlemen" or "Beware of Dog".

Half an hour before the start of the first race the name plate was glued to the transom. "Beware of Dog" proved she was no "woofer" by taking the championship with two wins and a second.

False move
TWO FARR ONE Tonners were reaching down the line in Hobart before a running start. The gun went, the leading boat bore off for the first mark and its stern smacked into the second Farr, to windward.

The skipper of the leading Farr did his nut! He began informing the windward boat crew in no uncertain terms that they were in the wrong. Then, to the amazement of his listeners, his harangue halted in mid flight when the skipper's false teeth popped out and clattered to the deck.

The captain was made of stern stuff. He bent down, picked up the recalcitrant teeth, re-adjusted them and carried right on from where he'd left off.

Right or wrong under the rules, his boat gained an immediate tactical advantage. The crew of the second boat was so helpless with laughter, they fell far behind.

Sheppo again

KEVIN SHEPHARD WAS once sailing in the famous Admiral's Cup at Cowes and somehow cracked an invitation to Sir Max Aitken's dinner, which always used to be a jolly and exclusive affair often attended by the Duke of Edinburgh and always, until his death, by Uffa Fox who would sing a song or two.

Sir Max's house is like a maritime museum and has some fine seascape paintings. Sheppo found himself seated opposite Baron de Rothshchild from the French team. And the Baron was seated under an enormous painting of the Battle of Trafalgar.

Feeling a mite overpowered by the company, our lad made a nervous stab at some polite conversation: "Er, it seems the greatest of ill taste, sir, to seat you under that painting."

The Baron: "I wouldn't worry too much about it; Aussie ... the bastards beat us again today."

Stan's stew

ON A VISIT to Melbourne I ran into Roger Smith, the Commodore of the Hobsons Bay Yacht Club and we began yarning about our strange and wonderful times at sea with Stan Gibson, who had died about 18 months previously.

We had many experiences to share because Roger and I sailed our first long ocean races with Stan aboard his 27-footer Four Winds; famous for many years as the smallest yacht in the Sydney-Hobart.

Stan gave dozens of wide-eyed youngsters, as we were in those days, their first chance to go ocean racing on Four Winds and the bigger yacht that he built to replace her, Four Winds II.

Stan never mastered the niceties of hot-shot IOR racing but he was a wonderful seaman. If you were caught in a gale with Stan, you knew boat and crew would come through.

He liked to live rough at sea, insisted on doing the cooking and you needed a strong stomach to cope with his famous stew. The recipe was to fire up the stewing steak in the pot with some spuds and onions and stuff the day of the start and keep it going for the duration, adding curry powder as the brew became aromatic. Constipation was an unknown complaint on Four Winds I and II.

Roger took me down to Hobsons Bay YC to show me a board to Stan's memory, carrying many of the race plaques from his long career – about 104 major ocean races from his first with the little Four Winds in 1956.

Roger Smith with the memorial board to Stan Gibson at Hobsons Bay Yacht Club

Hobsons Bay was Stan's home club, most of its offshore members did their first racing with Stan and it was his wish that the race plaques went back to the club after his death. The memorial board is a nice tribute; I only wish they had found a corner on it for a simmering stew pot.

Holding the baby

THE NIGHT BEFORE the last race of the elimination series for the 1982 J24 world championship in Sydney, one of the Australian skippers tarried overlong at the Middle Harbour Yacht Club, celebrating the completion of heat six.

Realising sensibly that he was in no condition to drive home, he wandered aboard his J24 at the marina and slept there.

Next morning, as he and his crew were preparing to cast off to go racing, his wife materialised dockside holding their baby in a bassinet.

I won't swear to the exact wording, but she said something like: "Here, it's your turn to mind him" and walked off to spend the day at the beach with some girl friends.

Our hero took it in good part. He missed the race but she had left him some nappies and a spare bottle or two. He did qualify for the worlds and even volunteered the story to me.

Another good one from the J24 worlds came to me from Doug Brockhoff, an Australian competitor and class association measurer.

Brockhoff, who had built something of a reputation as a sailing litigant, noticed the name "Alitalia" going onto the side of an Italian entry for the world championship. He wandered over and had his say to the crew about Rule 26 (thou shalt not carry advertising on thy boat).

One of the Italians pointed to the skipper and said, "Well his name is Al … and he is from Italy!"

Brocky obligingly drew in a full point, in red Textacolor, between Al and Italia. There were other forces at work, however and next day the "Al" had disappeared, leaving the Italians to race a boat called Italia.

America's Cup loonies

There's something about the America's Cup that brings them out of the basketwork: A pleasant-sounding young lady from an advertising agency rang the other day after some America's Cup pictures for a big presentation.

She said she wanted as many boats as possible in the picture and sounded surprised when we explained to her that the America's Cup is a two-boat race.

It reminded me of a biography of John Bertrand, circulated by a public relations company a year or two ago, which listed among his many successes: "Second, America's Cup 1970". Might make a good tee shirt or blazer pocket.

Other characters are looking for a rails run on the America's Cup Twelves. I ran into a laid-back tow-haired youngster from the Whitsundays who applied to the Bond syndicate for a try-out and gave as his principal reasons for applying: "I've always wanted to sail on a great big boat and I hate Yanks."

The Bond syndicate, which is not without humour, replied with thanks and said they had put him on the "long list" of applicants.

'Don't shoot!'

Seven-year-old Andy tried to stow away on Wonoka for the Adelaide-Port Lincoln race, to be with his dad who was in the crew and because he reckoned he could steer the boat as well as anyone, having learned all about the compass at Scouts.

He hid under a bunk while his parents searched frantically for him ashore, until the penny dropped. His mother climbed aboard the boat, heard a rattle and said: "I think you've got rats on this boat but don't worry, I've got a gun and will deal with them."

"Don't shoot," said Andy as he materialised. He did get to see the start from a motor boat and has been promised a ride on the return cruise aboard the boat next year.

Hobart hitch-hiker

As the mighty Apollo motored back up Sydney Harbour an hour or two after losing the end of her main boom soon after the start of the 1981 Sydney-Hobart race Sandy Schofield, who had laboured long and hard on the boat, was wondering what he was going to do about his wife and children, who were on their way to meet him in Hobart for a Tasmanian holiday together after the race.

About then, Norman Rydge's magnificent motor cruiser (young ship, really) Koomooloo came down harbour on its way to following the fleet to Hobart and some friends of Sandy's on board gave him a wave.

Always a quick thinker, Sandy shot below, re-appeared on deck with his gear bag and flagged down Koomooloo. A brief goodbye and a giant leap later, he was on his way to Hobart in comfort and with no worries about going to windward.

Hooked, line and sinker

WINTER RACING ON Sydney Harbour can be both relaxing and terrifying at the same time, mixing as it does a variety of boats under crews of varying skills.

Understandably, none of the principal players in the following drama saw anything funny in it but those in the front stalls on nearby boats were in stitches:

The maxi Vengeance, on starboard, was charging up Rose Bay at 8.25 knots when it called a port-tack Bounty 35, which obediently tacked. However, the quarters were close enough for the main boom topping lift on Vengeance to hook around the 35's mast and in no time, the 35 was creaming along behind Vengeance, sideways, at a similar 8.25 knots.

David Kellett, skipper of Vengeance, fired the clip on the boom end of the topping lift, at risk of shredding his finger, but this just sent the end of the topping lift lassoing around the 35's mast to form an even more secure towing hitch. Finally, the topping lift was cut at Vengeance's mast end and the tow terminated.

I believe there was a certain amount of tension later when Kellett went around to the 35 and asked for his topping lift back. But happily, no great damage was done to boat or people.

Buster gift-wraps Bradley's

ONE INCREDIBLE TALE always tends to uncover another. The item about Vengeance lassoing and leg-roping a Bounty 35 with her main boom topping lift led to a string of similar tails at that fountain of knowledge and good beer, the members' bar of the Middle Harbour Yacht Club.

Buster Brown, who has experienced almost everything the sailing life has to offer, topped and halted the whole debate with the tale of how a Soling spinnaker "gift-wrapped" the Bradley's Junction mark in Sydney Harbour.

Buster was aboard the Soling when the spinnaker flopped over the mark.

Buster Brown, Middle Harbour legend

He jumped onto the mark to race up the ladder inside and try to free the kite from the top.

Brace, sheet and halyard were let go but, as Buster tells it, the Soling just kept going around the mark, steadily winding itself in on the lines of the spinnaker and imprisoning Buster within an eerie, multi-coloured shroud of spinnaker cloth.

The boat finally stopped a foot or so from this large navigational mark and Buster was able to free the kite from the spiky top without even a tear. Amazing? I thought so, but ask him yourself.

Police Car's pink erection

THE MORNING OF the 775n miles around-the-state race of the 1982 Clipper Cup, it was raining and well-known Australian wine maker Sir James Hardy had to buy a bottle of cheap rose to complete a finishing touch to the repaired mast of Police Car. It was the only way he could find a cork to plug the sail track and stop rainwater running below.

Jim had put in four solid days of dawn-to-midnight work repairing the mast, broken in the second race, at the yacht engineering shop of Timmy Rhea. Tim, a super-relaxed guy, was recovering from a leg injury and directed operations from his barber's chair near the front door often, in the evenings, with a tall glass of rum and pineapple juice in his hand.

The repaired mast re-appeared on the boat with the bottom section strangely painted nipple pink. Towards the end of the mast-repair epic Jim, some of his crew and Timmy's boys had reached item 14 of a very detailed specification for the repair written by Police Car's designer Ed Dubois.

It read: "If time, paint pink" (meaning etch primer). Well it was late at night, a few Bacardi golds and cans of Bud had gone down and everybody thought it was a good idea when Timmy reached for that pink auto enamel he had on the shelf and loaded his spray gun.

Tim Rhea became so busy, repairing boats busted in this heavy-air series, he was unable to observe the racing he had planned aboard the yacht X-rated with a bunch of lovely young girls and his good friend Bamboo Opperman, a wonderful local character with a liking for the practical joke.

Bamboo was once facing a vital pointscore race in Cal 20s. He laid the suitable wagers the night before with his closest opponent and busied himself with other matters.

When opponent and crew arrived at the Waikiki Yacht Club to go racing the next morning, they found their boat floating in the swimming pool.

The best one-liner of the series came from Police Car helmsman Freddy Neill. Driving back to Honolulu from a party on the other side of the mountains that divide Oahu, Fred was making some nervous observations about the speed of the old truck and its apparent lack of brakes.

Hawaiian boatyard wisdom at the 1982 Clipper Cup

The friendly local driver just said: "We are here for a good time ... not for a long time."

Ace's road-story epic

ACE MOWTELL'S DEEDS with his big needle-nosed yellow camera boat are passing into folklore as rapidly as his photography, but have you heard about his latest epic?

He was invited to photograph the Whitsunday Fun Race, where each competing yacht features a topless "Miss Fun Race" figurehead. Never being one to avoid a well-structured female chest, Ace decided to tow his boat north.

He went to untold trouble to ensure that its radio whip aerial would pass safely underneath the bridges along the way; ascertaining such detail as the 4.9m clearance at Wyong and 4.7m at Maclean. Then, powering off at the very start of his journey, he snapped off the aerial on an overhanging tree branch at Double Bay.

Night watch trivia

I NEVER CEASE to be amazed at the amount of sheer trivia that flows in an endless stream on the night watches of a long ocean race. From life stories to lewd jokes, they mostly flow in one ear and out the other in my head, making little impression on whatever is left in there by many years of decadent living.

But the following exchange on an off-watch was so remarkable for its twists and turns that I sat bolt upright in my bunk and immediately wrote it down:

It began when the navigator killed a cockroach that happened to be heel-

and toeing straight the rhumb line on his chart.

"Did you know," said the skipper, who has an endless fund of such useless information and so is in demand as an after-dinner speaker, "that cockroaches are so prevalent in New York that when kids in schools are asked to draw something from their home life, they draw the roaches every time; they are like family pets."

"They're hard to get rid of on a boat, but not as hard as the rats. My brother once had a rat come aboard a yacht he was delivering to Hawaii in Suva. They couldn't catch it and it drove them mad."

Navigator: "That reminds me of the time a bush rat got on board Janzoon while she was slipped at North Harbour. It got into the lockers, ate the tapes off Doug Brown's sou'-wester, chewed a hole through a jumper and a hole through the head of a spinnaker.

"We didn't find out about that until we set it in a Deep Freeze race. That was the first nylon spinnaker Joey Pearce made; fortunately it missed the tapes."

Skipper, not to be outdone: "Do you know that on one of the islands where they had the A-bomb tests the rats have 100 per cent more radio-activity than any human could withstand. It makes them so tough, they can chew through six inches of concrete."

Impressionable youngest member of the crew: "Super rats take over the world! It's like a space movie – Far out!"

Low-tech end to high-tech 18

PICTURED ARE THE remains of the 18-footer Breville Cyclonic Whizz which, I trust, have since been quietly laid to rest by their owner, Michael Spies, who is an undertaker.

In the last moments of this hard-worked craft, fourth in the successful Color 7 lineage of Iain Murray: Breville was running under spinnaker from the Beashel Buoy, past Nick Scali, which had just capsized and close to Bradmill, so the heat was on. The nose dug in to a gust and Spies pulled the boat away.

The next voice heard in the boat was the loud one, of Steve ("Mothball") Jarvin: "Cripes mate, we're in trouble." He was watching the front two metres of the boat breaking away.

Spies to Moth: "Don't let the spinnaker sheet go."

Sheet hand Charlie ("The Messiah") Diekman, so called

Remains of Breville Cyclonic Whizz ready to be laid to rest after her final 18ft skiff race, 1983

because he went from 21st to first last year in a heat of the Interdominion 12ft skiff championship on a miraculous wind change, could only manage: "I pass."

BC Whizz was beyond salvation. It planed on for another 200 metres with the whole bow flapping loose like a sole parting company with a worn shoe, before it gurgled down.

The high-tech hull was probably hastened to its low-tech ending by the trip across the Nullabor and back for the Australian championship in Perth a few weeks earlier.

As if punctures and blowouts were not enough, the trip was made longer than it need be. Approaching Norseman on the way back, Spies felt sleepy. He handed the wheel to the co-driver with instructions to be woken at Balladonia, 75km farther on. He awoke, amazed at the progress the town had made since his last passage, before realising they were in Esperance, on the coast, about 75km off course.

Blackaller on solo racing

I LIKE AND agreed with the comment of Tom Blackaller, the flambouyant American who will be helming Defender in the US America's Cup defence eliminations, on the BOC Challenge single-handed race around the world: "It bears about as much resemblance to yacht racing as climbing the World Trade Tower does to mountain climbing."

Below with Benny – by Bob Ross

THE DAY AFTER the Westpac series, a warm-up for the Australian challengers on Port Phillip for the 1983 America's Cup, I am sitting below in the "sewer" of Australia II and feeling distinctly nervous.

I am trying for the fourth day in a row to interview designer Ben Lexcen on what he thinks of the form of his two new Twelves in the Westpac series. Australia II the previous day had won the final race over a full 24.5n mile America's Cup course. In their four meetings during the previous heats over half-size America's Cup courses the score was two-all. I am keen to get Ben's reaction to the result.

At last I have cornered the mercurial Benny but he is pre-occupied with a peculiar problem. The hydraulic ram that tensions Australia II's rig by lifting the mast step has blown a seal, leaving the mast jammed in the fully-tensioned position. The mast has to come out so that the boat can be packed up for the USA. There is no way of reaching the faulty ram which is enclosed in the mast.

Ben with some temporary hydraulic jacks is trying to lift an edge of the mast far enough to remove blocks supporting it. While support-group

Ben Lexcen dances for joy in the new trainers issued to the crew of Australia II during the 1983 warm-up trials in Melbourne

member Steve Harrison pushes and pulls at the runners and deck-level mast ram to rock the bottom of the mast, Ben belts away at the blocks with a hammer.

Somehow it seems to be the wrong time to be questioning him about the sophisticated design and engineering features – including a revolutionary and still secret keel – of what has been hailed as the most potent and best-prepared challenger of all time.

But as Ben hammers, I persist. How did he feel about the outcome of the Westpac series? "It confirms my confidence in this boat but the other one is better than I thought it would be."

When would he show the world the tricky keel? "We are even going to hide it in America, keep a bag around it to keep the opposition worrying about it. You see, even if they knew what it is like, they wouldn't know if we had changed it."

In performance terms, what was it doing for the boat? "The boat goes faster, it does not go sideways as much; it allows the boat to sail more upright."

More hammering. "Have you got the bigger jack, Steve? Shoot it down here."

It does seem you are the only designer with something different. "The other guys have tried different things haven't they and they have not been able to get them to work. We might have it working; we don't know."

Gordon Ingate, owner-skipper of Gretel II joins us. He is an engineer and marvels at what Ben is trying to do. Jokingly, he offers to lend Ben some bolt cutters to snip a shroud and relieve the tension on the rig.

Ben: "Who would cut it? Who would be game enough to? Where would you end up when it went? Whooo… the mast would end up over the other side of the shipyard and the bloke the other side of the car park somewhere."

By now Steve has pushed the mast all the way forward with the deck-level ram and loaded the runners to the point that the mast, through the open hatch above us, looks like an archer's bow just before the arrow is loosed.

Ben tells us there is 57,000 lb of tension on the rigging. "There is more load on the mast right now than the weight of the boat. The rig has stretched three inches."

Lexcen says he is thankful that Gretel II, the promising challenger of 1970 and campaigned again in 1977, had competed in Melbourne. "Before Gordon came down here I was really depressed, starting to get second thoughts; maybe I'm mad maybe they're both a couple of dogs.

"Gordon did pretty good. They are not dogs, they are in the right area. Maybe they're better, maybe they're worse.

"I know from our tests that Challenge 12 is faster than our old boat (Australia, 1980 challenger). It is faster upwind in light weather but only microscopically, 10sec on a beat. But in a breeze that boat is much faster than our old boat. Its righting moment is heaps up on the old boat." He adds that Australia II is probably another 10 per cent stiffer than Challenge 12.

Ingate remarks that Challenge 12 had passed Australia II downwind. Ben comments: "It's spinnakers. In the tank, this boat has exactly the same drag and that is the most reliable thing in the tank that you can do. On the wind, this one is definitely better; there is no doubt of it in my mind.

"It has the manoeuvrability aspect, which is a big plus if you can use it right. The tacking and acceleration of this boat is superior."

Ingate: "We did three tacks with them and they gained a minute."

Lexcen: "Acceleration is like a rocket."

More hammering and the whole boat groans. Ben to Steve: "Yeah, the mast's right forward; just let the runners off and pump the forestay down as far as it will go. I think we will get it out Steve."

I exchange glances with Ingate and sense that he, too, is looking for a decent excuse to leave. But I stay. This is only time Ben has been in one spot for more than five minutes in a week.

What is the displacement of Australia II? "I'm not telling you. It is lightish and the boat is fairly long. This boat has long sailing length and short waterline and so is a light boat. We have no bustle and a dinghy rudder. It feels like a dinghy to sail too. It does not feel like a Twelve Metre, it feels like a dinghy. It has the responses of a dinghy. If you pull it away, it accelerates straight away.

Ingate: "Do you see what Alan Payne is getting at with Advance?"

"No, it is just bloody odd. I think he has tried to make the hull generate side force. I don't think that's the way to go when you can make keels so efficient.

"We did (theoretical) tests, segmenting the boat into three sections. The front of the boat has something like 10 per cent of the lift. The middle of the boat where the keel is, like 90 per cent and the back of the boat where the bustle is has negative lift. It pushes the boat to leeward. That's why I took the bustle off."

"*A-frame coming aft, forestay off first.*" *The boat groans a loud sigh of relief in a key that Lexcen says is A-flat.*

He tries to re-assure us. "I put safety factors like one and a-half and two into critical things like chainplates and things low down where the weight doesn't count and up high I put minus safety factors."

"Has the mast come aft?"

"Not enough to get it off this thing, I can tell you that."

"Can you rake it some more?"

"Is that ram right out and pull the runners on a bit"

Lexcen, hammering at the block: "I'll get this out if I get the f...ing Nobel Peace prize for engineering in pieces."

"BANG!" One of the minus safety factors has had enough. The adjustment thread on a spreader base breaks. With a tremendous bang that has shell-shocked Twelve Metre crewmen all over the dockside area ducking for cover, the rig frees itself from the torturing hydraulics.

There is relief all round. "Good," says Lexcen. "Now we can get the mast out." The crew is pleased because they now cannot take part in a public-relations sailpast of the boats along the St Kilda foreshore. I am pleased just to be able to walk away.

Boat hits car

INSURANCE IS HARDLY a laugh-a-minute business but the sailors at City Mutual were holding their sides after receiving the following claim (first related by Bert Wholohan in the Hartley TS16 newsletter):

"Last Saturday, after sailing training, I had a small accident with my yacht, a TS16 (trailer sailer). While towing it up the beach at the sailing club, the jib sheet fell overboard and got wound around one of the trailer wheels. This pulled the sail on hard and made the boat sail up the beach even after my car stopped towing it (by a long rope). I ran back and tried to stop it but this was impossible.

"The boat was heading for two parked cars, a Mercedes Benz and a Ford Falcon. As I figured the Falcon would be cheaper to repair, I pushed the bow away from the Mercedes and the tow bar of the trailer pushed in the stone guard under the Falcon's bumper bar.

"I told the car owner that I would advise my insurance company about the accident. I would also like to make a claim under my insurance policy for a new jib sheet because the one I had was ruined and snapped when it wrapped around the wheel."

Cruising companion pets

A CORRESPONDENT FROM Royal Papua New Guinea Yacht Club tells me that hermit crabs are not unusual pets on cruising boats visiting Port Moresby. One such crab lived in a shoe. Many a visitor stopped quietly sipping a drink (or rapidly downed the lot) at the sight of a claw emerging and waving from an old sandshoe on the cabin sole.

Another hermit crab named Spike, after leaving Port Moresby on Sea Lark, travelled to California and settled down for a few weeks in the rolling country north of Los Angeles, subsisting happily on rice and pasta, which he preferred to meat.

He survived a long trip that followed, to New Zealand, but in Wellington passed away during a sudden onset of bleak weather (having been born in the place, I completely understand).

Another couple kept a goat as a cruising companion. That was all very well when it first arrived as a tiny fluffy ball, looking more like a kitten.

Unfortunately, when it grew up it developed an insatiable appetite for varnish. Olga and Rudi realised it had to go when it began to eat the companionway ladder. A "Doctor Doolittle" at Mooloolaba, whose small property is a haven for unwanted geese, dogs and ponies, now owns one large and happy goat. I love those cheerful endings.

Spit Bridge race

THEIR EYES MET at ten minutes to go. The friendship and respect forged through years of sailing with and against each other gave way to the ruthless, uncompromising cunning of competition.

The idle circling became more purposeful as the countdown progressed and took them through or around the 25 boats watching and waiting.

Finally, the sound signal. On a perfect layline and at full speed, the little PR25 cruiser-racer won the start in the race under motor to be first through the opening Spit Bridge on Sydney's Middle Harbour, metres clear of his opponent in the J24.

"He can't help himself," said his J24 mate. "He has got to win and let you know that he has won. He went through the bridge at such a rate that we never caught up.

"But that night I was at a party when this call came through for me from someone purporting to be the Spit Bridge operator, claiming I had infringed some rule or other. It was just Bruce, who had gone to untold trouble to track me down, doing a nice job with a false voice, but really just rubbing it in."

Adversity's reward

A SCRAP OF gold can sometimes be mined from a mountain of adversity. John Messenger, an insurance assessor for Marine Hull, told me the sad story of the loss of a round-the-world dream yacht on the Southport Bar.

Five young Melbourne fellows clubbed together to buy the ferro-cement yacht in Mooloolaba and the father of one of them, with a companion, was delivering it to Melbourne.

While crossing the Southport Bar, the keel hit the bottom and in seconds the yacht was wrecked. The crew saved themselves but little else, losing among other possessions three wallets.

When the wreck was dragged ashore by bulldozer, the father dug through the sand inside the cabin and found two wallets but the third, containing a large sum of money, was missing.

Finally came the saddest moment of all. Stripped of all salvageable gear, the remains of the hull had to be broken up. As the bulldozer lifted the hull and began turning it over, the third wallet plopped out of the bulldozer blade onto the sand.

The whistling oyster

THROUGH THE ASSISTANCE of Ron Holland, the New Zealand yacht designer who conducts his international operation from an ancient farm house (the design office is actually an extension of the pig pen) in Cork, Ireland, I got out to the Fastnet Rock to see the 1983 Admiral's Cup fleet go round.

Ron arranged a ride for me on a handsome 43ft ketch, strangely named Whistling Oyster. It was owned by Bernie Cahill, Admiral of the Royal Cork Yacht Club, which is acclaimed as the oldest yacht club in the world (founded 1720).

Bernie explained the name. He wanted to include the word oyster and had a researcher in the grog business (Bernie's company among other things gave the world Bailey's Irish Cream) come up with the following legend:

"A whistling oyster created a lot of attention as well as a lot of custom to a certain London oyster house in 1840. The landlord separated the tuneful one from its fellows and placed it in a tub to itself where its continued performance drew streams of spectators.

"Among them was the novelist Thackeray who recorded that while he was there, an American arrived who said that this feat was nothing to an oyster he knew in Massachusetts which not only whistled 'Yankee Doodle' right through but followed its master around the house like a dog.

"This is only capped by the story of the man who boasted that he owned a tame clam which squirted jets of water in time to the national anthem."

At the America's Cup

THE PEOPLE WHO descended on Newport for the (1983) America's Cup this time, including my good self, have been rich in variety and number. In the midst of the extravaganza, the clerk at the American Express office for the region, a tiny outpost in a small town near here, was confronted by an unassuming character who casually requested $5000 in cash against his credit card.

The clerk dutifully dialled up whoever has to be called on to arbitrate on such things. "Describe him," said the voice. The clerk eyeballed the customer and gave the necessary rundown. "Pay him," said the voice. "You're looking at the Aga Khan."

Thereafter anyone going into that Amex office for a cash transaction was asked routinely, "How many thousands would you like?"

Australia's only (or at least most obvious) member of the New York Yacht Club, Gordon Ingate, did his best to persuade any Aussie in Newport who would listen that the NYYC were really a nice bunch of chaps.

One he did not manage to convince was Alan Bond. Each morning on race days Ingate had to walk down a dock outside the Australia II office to join a spectator boat.

Each morning he wore a New York Yacht Club cap. Finally, one day Bond could stand it no longer. He threw down Ingate's cap and jumped on it, 18 times.

The Australians, besides many broken hearts, left behind a new saying around the Newport docks. American workers were mystified a common call from Australia II's crew for "Beasho" (the AII maintenance chief Ken Beashel, in immediate demand whenever a problem arose).

"What's a 'Beasho'?, the Americans asked. "It means 'Fix it,'" said the Australians.

So whenever anyone wants anything fixed around Newport from now on, they just holler, "Beasho!"

The America's Cup dragged on for so long that spectators too engrossed to leave were reduced to sleeping on floors around Newport as their hotel bookings ran out, sending home for more money, thinking of new excuses for employers and forgetting who they really were.

One such, a British follower of Victory '83 who, like many others, transferred his support to Australia II for the Cup, said it for all: "I have been away from the office so long, I can't remember what we do there!"

The most telling card in the psychological pack for the Australia II crew in Newport was The Red Card. This little number, a piece of cardboard wrapped in red tape, felt-pen inscribed with "Have a Nice Day" and a smiling face was awarded to any member of the crew who "spat the dummy" (lost his temper) aboard the boat.

It would be awarded with due ceremony before the whole crew assembled aft with the recipient standing on top of the mainsheet pedestal, usually in full view of the tender. The card had to be worn until someone else was deemed worthy of its receipt.

The Red Card was devised by Rob Brown, one of the sail trimmers, early in the challenger eliminations, as a way of easing tensions on the boat. First recipient was skipper John Bertrand, who sounded off at Brown for the way he was trimming the genoa on a particularly frustrating light day. Brown rushed up the card overnight, it was presented to Bertrand next day and from there was a marvellous influence on the whole crew; defusing tense situations quickly with a joke.

One of the more startling award-winning incidents occurred in a race against France 3 when the wind socked in to 30 knots. Peter Costello went forward to help secure a genoa and while he was making his way back aft, Sir James Hardy, helming for the day, saw a big wave coming along the deck and called: "Watch yourself, you could get washed off the boat."

To which the normally mild-mannered giant of an Army major replied, "You do your job, I'll do mine."

Sir James was to be red-carded himself. Initially the card did not go beyond the gunwales of Australia II. But as the crew became steadily calmer during the Cup races, the group on the tender Black Swan became commensurately uptight and so, decided the crew, needed the card.

Sir James was red-carded after the US defender Liberty, still on the wind, tried to "nail" Australia II running away from the windward mark in race six, for calling across to Commodore Robert McCullough on the nearby motor yacht carrying members of the New York Yacht Club's America's Cup committee, "That is the most blatant violation of Rule 35.1 that I have ever seen."

The one question that remained unasked at the final press conference was why Warren Jones, executive director of the Australia II syndicate, was wearing the red card. I am reliably informed that it was for words he hurled at Gordon Ingate, an Australian member of the New York Yacht Club, as Australia II, towing in after winning race seven to secure the America's Cup, passed the vast cruising yacht Scotch Mist bearing Gordon among other NYYC members.

Jones, inspired by a couple of glasses of champagne, took the opportunity to answer some of the helpful advice and opinions on their chances Gordon had been offering the Australia II syndicate in Newport.

I cannot repeat the words used as I do not wish to be stuck with wearing The Red Card until the America's Cup 1987.

Tell-tail tale

MOST OF YOU have sailed with someone like this. You're at the helm, doing your best to concentrate on steering upwind and this guy on the rail keeps on and on:

"You're too high ..." "Now you're too low ..." "Oh for Pete's sake you're way too high."

"Too low; how the hell do you ever expect us to get to the mark" ... "Too high."

The absolute world champion of this breed is an Aussie who for the past few years has worked and sailed in the USA and who I hope and believe is heading this way for the Southern Cross Cup.

On a recent visit to the States, I was delighted to learn his new nickname: "The Human Tell-tail."

Quick fix

HOW'S THIS FOR a recovery: Brad Barker and crew of Port Curtis Sailing Club, Gladstone, dropped off the mooring and were 50 metres along the way to a start when the steering failed on their Serendipity 28. The weld of the tiller to the rudder stock had broken.

With the help of trusty multi-grips they steered to the closest moored craft, just 12 metres away, to contemplate the problem.

The skipper of that boat, a charter vessel called Cowboy, inquired about their predicament. In just 10 minutes, the rudder was removed, Cowboy's generator fired up, welding gear dragged on deck, broken joint re-welded, rudder re-fitted and take-off for the start resumed; all for the price of a bottle of rum.

Divine intervention

BILL CULVERWELL, PUBLICITY officer for the Hartley TS16 Association of Australia, besides noting that at the 20th annual general meeting of the pioneer trailable yacht class this year that 675 members were currently active in 600 boats, dipped into the archives for this story:

"When I joined the association, the Reverend Russell Fowler enjoyed racing his TS16 with the Drummoyne club each Saturday and often had lots of bother 'getting to the church on time' for the usual 6pm wedding. As any sailor knows, ALL weddings occur at 5pm or 6pm on Saturdays. Many is the time, it is said, the reverend solemnly joined couples of non-sailors together in wedded bliss while his hidden sailing shorts dripped little puddles around his feet.

"One day our fleet was sailing the downwind leg, tailenders in fresher wind closing up to form a solid bunch at the mark. The Reverend Fowler had inside position on a dozen boats.

"Although he called for buoy room, he knew from experience that the chances of getting it were very remote and the usual barging and scraping was about to commence.

"He looked at the skipper of the next boat and to convey his despair raised his eyebrows with open palms. The adjacent skipper mistook the gesture and shouted, 'Do it again, Russell and I'll protest you for outside assistance.'"

Harrowing Hobart tales

THE MOST HARROWING tale from the 1983 Hitachi Sydney-Hobart blue water classic was that of the arresting and famous lady sailor who successfully completed the course only to nearly founder in a bath tub.

Worn out from the race and the first welcoming wave dockside, she repaired to her motel room, locked the door, ran a bath and climbed in. All of this was so relaxing that she fell asleep.

A friend returning home a little later noticed water cascading over the motel balcony and realised something was amiss. She hammered on the door, got no response and called the manager.

They burst in to find the famous lady sailor sleeping, mouth just above water level and the room awash.

The manager was so relieved that he didn't have a tragedy on his hands that he took a reasonable view of the situation.

The lady sailor, however, had to pay a certain price. She had stuffed $1000 in cash – the contribution of the crew towards providoring the boat – into a sea boot. The boot was caught in the ebb tide from the bath. Dollar bills were floating all over the place and $275 of them disappeared forever; presumably over the balcony.

Then there was the story of the quite big and beautifully-prepared yacht whose owner had installed a stainless-steel cover for the compass just before the race. On the first day the crew could not figure out why they were reaching to Hobart and everybody else was beating.

Getting 1730 disorganised and disoriented sailors out of Hobart after the race was the usual yearly miracle performed by the patient staff of TAA and Ansett. I suppose everyone in the race at times has changed a flight booking after being caught up in just one more round.

I got together with Lynn ("Squeaks") Keep from Ansett to try and figure out the record holder in this department. She says the hands-down winner was "Oddy", a big Scandinavian gentlemen who could relocate your mast by himself if you asked him to.

Squeaks in her trademark swimsuit checking out the bags after the 1983 Sydney-Hobart race at the Ansett hut on Constitution Dock

Three years ago he missed 11 flights in three days. "He just sat there with us drinking beer," said Squeaks in the airline's dockside caravan.

[Footnote: After publication of the above, Oddy complained about its accuracy. He wants it known that he did not miss 11 flights in three days to set a record for trying and failing to get out of

Hobart. *The figure was actually 27: 15 with Ansett and 12 with TAA (he likes to spread the business).]*

The 1983 Hobart race was the one in which an close duel for line honours between Marvin Green's Nirvana and Bob Bell's Condor ended with Condor hitting White Rock, near the finish in the Derwent River, leaving Nirvana to slide by and get the gun 2min 16sec. But next day in the protest room, the jury disqualified Condor for failing to give Condor sufficient shore room.

Whatever ill-feeling there may have been between the two crews over the incident were laid to rest on New Year's Day. They chartered a ferry, loaded it with beer and a band and went back to White Rock where a minute's silence was observed and the band played "The Last Post".

720 record?
IF THIS ISN'T a record, it's dizzier than standing on a stereo turntable: During the Australian J24 championship, a boat that had best be identified as Disaster, fouled a competitor on the approach to a leeward mark.

While executing the exonerating 720-degree turn, Disaster hit the mark and so had to do a 360-degree penalty turn. Through the 360, it fouled a second competitor, necessitating a further 720.

Wait, there's more: Through the second 720, Disaster again hit the mark. With the tally at 2160 degrees of penalty turn, we leave Disaster which, for all I know, may still be trying to round that mark.

Isle of Wight French
NEWS THAT TONY ("Cobb") de Young is to again manage the Admiral's Cup team spun me back to a night on the Isle of Wight in 1983. After a long day on the race course and a long evening at the typewriter we sat with Tony, desperately trying to order a bottle of good wine to go with the hamburgers in a little Newport eatery.

After one disastrous selection, Tony put on his civilised mode of address to the personable young waitress:

"You have a comprehensive wine list but we are not too familiar with the French whites and need some help.

"Do you have a maitre d'?"

To which the waitress said: "I'm sure if we have it sir, it is on that list."

Very good restaurant
I AM REMINDED also by the presence in Sydney of the dynamic Dick Gooch, planning chairman of the Pan Am Clipper Cup series, of the time when Dick,

in Hong Kong for the China Seas race, turned to the Balmoral bon vivant Don Mickleborough and said: "I am going to take you to a very good restaurant."

Some minutes later, their taxi pulled up in Kowloon opposite an establishment bearing the sign, "A Very Good Restaurant."

Moreton Bay porridge

THERE HAS BEEN some debate lately from forums between the CYCA in Sydney and the Barefoot Bar on Hamilton Island over the origins and true nature of the Queensland delicacy known as Moreton Bay porridge.

I always believed, through my association with the Cavill family who seem to like the stuff, that Moreton Bay porridge was simply Bundaberg rum and milk, with ice for those who wanted to go upmarket.

Not so. Clemmie Masters, widely acclaimed as the inventor of this health food, tells me that the true Moreton Bay porridge in its original form was made with powdered milk. Add a spoonful of sugar and you had "home-made Kaluah," says Clem.

He recommended that you have one every time you passed a pile on Moreton Bay.

Funny boat names

I GAVE UP recording funny boat names in this column some time ago; there are just so many around. But I must pass this one along: Noolas Rab. Give up? The owner devised it while sitting in a Drummoyne pub, looking through a swinging glass door.

Curley Stalker, trouble shooter

"CURLEY", WHOSE REAL name I can reveal is David Stalker, has featured in this column before. It was he who became marooned on Clarke Island after trying to paddle a leaking canoe home after a big night at the Mosman Rowers. It was he who jumped/fell off a Dragon alongside the Hobsons Bay YC pier and became entrapped by his sea boots in the mud (almost a sad ending, that one).

Well, he has just returned from helping deliver a trawler to Southport with another one for the archives. On the way home, he decided to look up some mates at the Fraser sail loft in Brisbane. His visit happened to coincide with a meeting of the "Curry Club" at Bonaparte's, a lively watering hole that is practically a branch office of the club.

Curry Club members, who are dedicated to the hot stuff and whatever is needed to wash it down, are allowed to bring a guest provided that the guest is some sort of celebrity or business heavy. And so Curley was introduced as an "international yachtsman and professional trouble shooter".

The flourish at the end of that title prompted a serious response from one of the regular Curry Club members who obviously hasn't got the full biography on Curley (he's into making trouble rather than fixing it).

This guy seriously, asked Curley: "If you are a trouble shooter and know about boats maybe you can help me. I've got this problem with my 16-footer. A bull terrier keeps trying to chew the transom off it. What can I do?"

Curley's solution was: "Hang a leg of lamb from the bow. If that doesn't work, invest in a double-barreled shotgun."

Funny boat names book-closer
THE BOOK, I believe, has now been closed on funny boat names by the blind Victorian yachtsman and the psychiatrist who bought the Farr 37 "Leading Edge" and re-named it "Out of Sight, Out of Mind". But the following is still available: "The Waiter's Eye"; you know, something you can never catch.

Too true
THE PERPETUAL TROPHY for Hamilton Island Race Week, that mixture of first-class racing in warm tropical waters and fun ashore at the magnificent new Whitsunday Islands resort, is in keeping with the venue and the event.

It's a bronze model of Jack Rooklyn's maxi Apollo atop a wooden base flanked by two finely-carved dolphins. The creator of the trophy, a sculptor on the Gold Coast, might not have known a lot about yachts but, as a truly professional artist, he has a tremendous eye for detail and thoroughly researched the work.

While Apollo was on the slips at Lloyds Shipyard in the Brisbane River for one of her many alterations, he went along and studied her; took measurements and photographs.

And sure enough, the boat sailing along atop the trophy is truly Apollo, with cockpits, stanchions, winches and deck fittings in place; complete down to every detail – including a slipway cradle arm projecting above the starboard topsides.

Finger in the pie
HEARD AGAIN AND enjoyed again recently the one about the Sydney Harbour big-yacht racing stalwart who a few years ago passed on to the great regatta in the sky.

This powerful businessman used to like to relax completely on race days with his crew, would lunch on board with them beforehand with his favourite meat pies with lots of tomato sauce. He was famous for his skill at puncturing the crust of his pie with his forefinger to admit the sauce.

One Saturday he invited a visiting American merchant banker to sail aboard for the race. The visitor turned up at the Royal Sydney Yacht Squadron in immaculate whites; a little out of place among the faded King Gee shorts and Bond's penguin shirts of the crew. But he had raced at home, and everything was going well until came to the ritual of the pies.

He was handed one and the skipper said to the crewman in charge of the sauce, "The Yank wants some tomato sauce."

And to the American: "Here, quick, put your finger in it (meaning the pie crust, to admit the sauce)."

The thoroughly bemused American thrust his finger into the sauce bottle.

Rugged Hobart race, afloat and ashore

THE 1984 SYDNEY-HOBART race was one of the roughest with gale-force headwinds raising punishing seas on the first two days knocking out 106 of the 152 starters, so most of the après-race festivities were at the Sydney end.

As the stream of retiring yachts turned into a flood, the bar staff of the Cruising Yacht Club of Australia wearily began filling glasses again. "Jeez, Hobart's changed," was the one-liner from a crewman staggering ashore at the CYCA marina that best summed the situation.

Another I liked very much was from John ("Munno") Munson, coming on deck as Margaret Rintoul IV turned to run home before the southerly: "The nor'-easter has come in early today."

Seasickness is an abominable illness, not to be laughed at (but let's have a go anyway). A maxi took along a couple of eager television type people who quickly lost interest in the big race not long past Sydney Heads.

One of them distinguished himself by throwing up in the nearest available receptacle down below, which happened to be a pot of prawn/champignon/vegetable casserole on the galley stove. Even the cook, who is a lady with a very strong stomach, took a turn for the worse.

Down in Hobart, although the 46 finishers got the tremendous welcome they deserved from the local folk, things were beautifully peaceful and civilised around the usual watering holes.

The Royal Yacht Club of Tasmania volunteers manning the information box alongside the strangely empty Constitution Dock posted some penetrating messages: "See the yachts now – fly to Sydney."

And over the list of retirements: "AWA-RYCT real estate for rent – Constitution Dock, Elizabeth St Pier, very cheap!"

However, I will best remember this Hobart as the one in which Tony Cable, an original perpetrator and mainstay for 46 years of the Quiet Little Drink, finally got what he deserved for inflicting the same two jokes on this dubious gathering for those 16 years.

It seems that Cable got to know this senior Hobart policeman with a sense of humour while the policeman was visiting Sydney for a course at the police college. Realising that it was in the best interests of both to cooperate on the arrangements for the QLD, they arranged to meet beforehand in Hobart.

I was privileged to be part of that meeting, when the policeman dropped in on Cable and a few of us having lunch at a remote and beautiful location. During the course of what shall from henceforth be known as "the Quiet Little Lunch", Cable got carried away and began referring to the coppers as "blue heelers".

The senior policeman with sense of humour said: "If you call my blokes blue heelers, they will get your head in their hands and squeeze it 'til it goes pointy and your eyes bulge out."

Cable: "I'll look like a Tasmanian."

Innocent bystander: "You are bloody brave."

Next day, in view of the retirements, the QLD was quiet all right with the first half hour set aside for apologies. But it went along okay until mid-afternoon when the first sounds of breaking glass warned that the local youngsters, who had homed in on the Wheatsheaf, were getting out of hand.

Tony Cable entertains and is apprehended at the 1984 Quiet Little Drink in Hobart

That's when the senior policeman with a sense of humour played his trump card. Two plainclothes policeman stepped on stage, where Cable was in mid tap-dancing flight, handcuffed him and led him away over his plaintive protest, "You can't touch me, I'm from New South Wales."

The whole place went deadly quiet and order was restored. David Kellett of Vengeance, went down town to bail out Cable ... for $2; about the right price.

Murphy's Law

I GUESS ALL offshore sailors have gone through the frustrating business of having to thump torches to make them work. Just when you need the torch most, to find something or check the trim of a sail, it won't light up because of loose or corroded connections, or a plain old dose of Murphy's Law. So we have to sympathise with Bob Fraser, in the Hobart race aboard Bewinched. He was thumping and bashing away at his torch until, in sheer frustration, he tossed it overboard.

Wait for it; as soon as it hit the water it lit up beautifully.

Elvstrøm's ultimate tuning solution

PAUL ELVSTRØM, WINNER of a record four Olympic gold medals, pioneered the two-boat tuning approach. From his home near Copenhagen he would spend hours training in a Finn against tuning partners, believing that any one-design could be made to go faster than any other.

But there was this one Finn around that had something special about it. This boat became such an obsession with Paul that he finally bought it from its Swedish owner so that he could figure out how to beat it. He never managed to do that so, finally, he burnt it.

Kiernan's social sail

IF IAN KIERNAN, the BOC Challenge around-the-world racer, invites you to go for a bit of a social sail, read this story before replying:

Kiernan, as well as being a fine sailor, is a born wanderer. Since he bought the Tasman Seabird Maris from another great sailor and wanderer Jack Earl, he has cruised and raced – often single-handed – over just about all the Pacific there is between Sydney and San Francisco.

When Kiernan is in Sydney, Maris is usually to be found in Mosman Bay and Kiernan, in social hours, at that haven for water sportsmen, the Mosman Rowing Club ("the Rowers").

Another denizen of that watering hole is the "Bilge Rat". Bilge, whose real name is Peter Curran, fetched up in Mosman Bay about 20 years ago, not long after he arrived in Sydney from Tasmania. He stepped aboard the wrong ferry one day, thought Mosman Bay looked a lot more inviting than Manly and had a rowing club. He has been around that way ever since.

Ian Kiernan steering Maris, 1977

One quiet Monday, Kiernan said to Bilge: "What about coming for a sail?"

Bilge said, "Okay, but I will have to pick up my dry cleaning first."

With the garments still on their hangers, Bilge climbed aboard Maris with Kiernan. They sailed down Sydney Harbour, out to sea and on ... to Lord Howe Island where they stayed for four weeks.

'The Rat' explains

CHALLENGE III'S DISMASTING soon after the start of the Channel race in the 1985 Admiral's Cup was a shattering experience for all her crew – but especially so for Wayne ("The Rat") Dixon.

The Rat had gone forward to pull in the foot line on the number four jib. Challenge III dipped into a steep sea, putting him under water. When The Rat surfaced, he found Challenge III had no mast. Still holding the foot line, The Rat walked back down the deck and yelled apologetically. "I only pulled a string and I didn't think I pulled it that hard."

Chas sends Frizzle a cheerio

ANYONE WATCHING THE television coverage of Drum, upside down without a keel, in the 1985 Fastnet race, may have picked up a dishevelled, mustachioed figure waving gaily to the television cameras as he waited to be taken off the upturned hull by helicopter.

Well that was Chas from Tas, Charles Blundell, who next to Graham ("Frizzle") Freeman is Tasmania's most noted ocean racer (or maybe that should be the other way around).

Anyway Chas has that uncanny propensity to bob up in the right place at the wrong time ... he just had to be aboard Drum.

Apparently he was down below doing the dishes when, idly glancing out of the companionway, he noticed the Cornish coastline rotating in a strange way.

Chas quickly made his way out as Drum rolled over and clung to the rudder. And when he waved to the television chopper, he dedicated the signal to his old friend down south: "That's for Frizzle," he yelled, to the bemusement of the others clinging to the upturned hull.

Dorro's good advice

ANOTHER LOVELY ONE-LINER has come to my attention, uttered by that other legend in his own lunch-time, Leigh Dorrington, the Melbourne sailmaker. During the Olympic trials, in a tight situation on a starting line, the forward hand on another Soling began giving Dorrington a lengthy abusive mouthful.

Dorrington ended that by turning and shouting: "If I were you I'd get that nasty wound under your moustache stitched."

America's Cup campaigns

ON THE FAST-CHANGING face of Fremantle, preparing for the 1987 America's Cup, hotels appeared almost overnight and the watering holes appear to be more numerous than the customers to fill them.

Various ploys have been tried. The Sail and Anchor, besides having beers from all around the world on tap and in bottles began brewing its own – behind glass plate walls right in the bar. You can holler for more hops to be thrown in if you don't believe the brewmaster is doing the job.

The Fremantle, still under heavy renovation around the guests, tried that old standby, the topless barmaid. The Norfolk, an old pub lovingly restored, had folk singers in its outdoor courtyard.

But the most ambitious custom-builder attempt was that of the Auld Mug – a nicely restored hotel on High Street – favoured by the America II crew. Their support was understandable with their shore manager Jake Farrell a part owner of the hotel.

The management decided that a good old American arm-wrestling contest between Twelve Metre crewmen might bring in more business. And this it did until South Australian grinder Phil Dyer broke his arm in a contest with a New Zealander known as "Sledge". I don't know Sledge's real name but I do know that since the incident, which led to arm-wrestling being immediately discontinued, he has been re-named "Snap".

Among the many great one-liners to come out of Fremantle came from Buddy Melges of the Heart of America syndicate and from the tiny mid-west town of Zenda. On quitting a press conference in a hurry to fly home, he said: "I must return to Zenda. It's not the end of the world but you can see it from there."

Being prepared

TALK ABOUT BEING prepared! "Rigor Mortis" – real name John Vail who is a rigger by trade – was once more aboard Sagacious for the Sydney-Mooloolaba race.

A collision on the start line wiped out Sagacious' stanchions on one side. Not a problem for Mort. He just happened to have a set of spare stanchion bases in his gear bag and presto, the fence was quickly re-erected.

But he forgot his toothpaste.

Another story filtering back from the race that I liked was about the hot-shot helmsman, trying to straighten out some offshore newcomers, told the spinnaker trimmer to simply call "trim" instead of the laborious "wind it on" when he wanted help with the sheet.

The guy on the winch did not quite get the message. After ten minutes of "trim ... trim ... trim", he complained to the trimmer in an agitated way, "I wish you'd stop calling me 'Trim'. The name is Bruce."

Mobile One multiplies

I HAVE TO phrase this item from the 1986 Hamilton Island Race Week carefully as it involves the visionary Keith Williams who not only conceived the modern and beautiful Hamilton Island resort, but whose interest in boats and the people who sail them made him jump at accepting the Race Week concept.

Keith, when he is on the island, involves himself totally in the ongoing construction projects and the day-to-day running of the place. A yachtsman guest, who reported a faulty lock on the door of his apartment, had Keith turn up to fix it.

When he is on the move around the island in his four-wheel drive, Keith keeps his finger on the pulse by monitoring the traffic on the radio network that embraces about 50 stations in various vehicles, boats, planes and administrative offices. His call sign is "Mobile One".

Around seven one morning during Race Week, after a lot of radio chat on the network, a bemused voice cut in mysteriously with: "Everyone on this island is to slow down by quarter of an hour."

Keith, who was on the move, heard the transmission and pinched in: "This is Mobile One. Get off the air unauthorised station or you will be put off the island."

To which the bemused but quick-thinking unauthorised voice responded: "All stations, this is Mobile One, take no notice of transmission purporting to come from Mobile One for the next half hour."

The real Mobile One: "Unauthorised station, please identify."

Dead silence. But I'm told that people near radios all over the island were quietly cracking up and the pace did indeed slow for quarter of an hour.

Our man returned to his bunk, satisfied with the morning's work. But on awakening, sobered, he reviewed the situation and decided it was time for the NBO.

He packed and quietly left the island, his identity never revealed despite forceful enquiries from Keith Williams at the time.

Tony Cable eventually put his hand up as the unauthorised Mobile One on the death of Keith Williams in 2011.

Midwinter Murphy's law winner

MIKE WELSH'S ENTRY in Bob Cranse's mid-winter Murphy's law contest concerns the Dubois Half Tonner Madmen's Woodyard in the race of the Petersville regatta on Port Phillip:

"On waking in a fair state of disrepair after a heavy night at the Portsea pub, we sent a crew member up our newly-installed mast to tighten the jumpers. One turnbuckle broke in half, leaving the topmast uncontrollable.

"At the same time another crew member swimming under the boat noticed that the previously repaired rudder had again developed a large crack. Despite these setbacks, the intrepid crew decided to race, hoping everything would hold together.

"After cleverly manoeuvring for a great start, we tacked early for clear air and were immediately swept onto the start buoy by the out-going tide. That meant there were only 200 boats in front.

"At the first mark, the tide had most boats tricked with the result that a 40-footer charged into our stern, removing most of the pushpit and generally improving the ventilation down below. Still, we continued to gain a glorious 33rd.

"No-one felt like joining in the after-race festivities so we sailed directly back to Sandringham. After dropping the sails, we found the motor refused to go into gear. The gear box was full of water and has had to be reconditioned.

"So we hoisted the number three and proceeded to tack up to our pen in light airs. During this manoeuvring, a crew member managed to lock the sheet around the winch, causing the helmsman to lose all steerage and the yacht went up on the rocks of SYC's breakwater, leaving a large scar on the bow.

"Another yacht returning from Portsea towed us off and to our pen, where we quickly quit the yacht before we broke the thing in half.

"The final straw came on Monday when we slipped the boat and found that both propeller blades had dropped off. At that stage, any reasonable offer would have been accepted."

Troppo News gems

My absolutely all-time favourite club magazine is Cairn's YC's Troppo News which, besides providing a very comprehensive run-down on club news and sailing up north in general, has the most atrocious jokes. Example:

"Cannibals had captured two cruising yachties and were stewing them in a cauldron. The chief asked the cook, 'Why did you cut off their heads first?'

"I had to; they were eating all the potatoes."

And it has items other yachting journals miss, like:

"Mr William Smith of Norfolk sailed from Scotland to Great Yarmouth. Showing great independence of mind, en route he missed Bridlington Harbour by 400 yards and rammed a jetty.

"At Yarmouth he overshot by 90 miles and ran aground off Kent. A full-scale search for the boat was hampered by the change in its appearance. When it left Scotland, it was black with one mast. When rescued, it had two masts and was painted green. 'I passed the time while I was aground re-decorating,' Mr Smith explained.

"Entering Yarmouth Harbour, he scraped a floating museum, collided with a small coaster and hit an entrant in the Tall Ships race. He also knocked several guard rails off a trimaran and got the ropes of the cargo vessel Grippon wrapped around his mast.

"Describing the voyage as 'pleasant, with no hassles or worries,' Mr Smith said he planned on sailing to Australia next."

Let's hope he's heading for Cairns and not Sydney Harbour.

1986-1996

America's Cup preparations, 1986
DURING THE AMERICA'S Cup in Fremantle two members of Italia's crew, enjoying some rest days, reportedly jumped into a four-wheel drive and headed for the outback. Ripping along a back road, they suddenly had their first encounter with that unique Aussie road hazard, the kangaroo. The impact left their vehicle intact but the kangaroo prone, presumably dead.

The experience, the Italians felt, was worth recording on film. So they propped the kangaroo against a tree and to add colour to the Kodachrome dressed him in one of their Gucci jackets, a cap and sunglasses.

Satisfied with the effects, the cameraman took aim and ... to his amazement, the kangaroo slid out of focus and hopped smartly away, still wearing the cap, the sunglasses, the Gucci jacket containing a wallet full of dollars, credit cards and membership cards.

There were no reports later of a well-dressed, free-spending kangaroo propping up the bar in the exclusive ($3000 membership fee) Casa Italia club for syndicate members and supporters.

Curly Brydon's monument
CURLY BRYDON – newspaperman, World War Two flying ace, motor-racing driver and ocean-racing yachtsman – passed away in 1986 after packing several wonderful lifetimes into one.

My tribute is to his sense of fun, which in his younger days was positively lethal, especially when he was sailing aboard Rupert Murdoch's Ilina with such cohorts as Raw Meat, Thunder and the eternally playful Don Mickleborough.

Curly and Murdoch, who was still on the bottom rungs of his climb up the mega-media ladder, engineered the famous Ondine party at Constitution Dock in 1962.

Every other big Sydney-Hobart race yacht in the dock had thrown a party but Ondine's owner Huey Long, as sparse on fun as he was flush with dollars, showed no sign of reciprocating.

Rupert and Curly decided Ondine should have a party anyway. Long

Delphine waltzing with Don Mickleborough

was away in Launceston trying to round up evidence for a protest, so Mickleborough had a relation up there send a telegram in Long's name to Sven Joffs, Ondine's paid skipper, to make the boat ready for a party.

Rupert and Curly had beautifully embossed invitations printed: "You are invited to a small informal party aboard Ondine, drinks 8pm." And they delivered hundreds of them all over Hobart: Waterside workers, firemen, hospital staff ... all were invited, with wives.

The conspirators then organised 18-gallon kegs of beer (those were the days), set them up all around the dock, with the word that Ondine herself was out of bounds. The party was a great success. The Lord Mayor turned up and apparently enjoyed himself.

Huey Long, however, was furious. When he heard about the party, he tried to charter a plane to leave Tasmania.

Curly was just getting out of that one when another Hobart race rolled around and he proposed to Mickleborough that they go up town and buy up all the available water pistols with the impeccable reasoning: "No one can shoot us and we can shoot anyone."

But they got side tracked by a stunning display in the window of Delphine's dress shop. They decided to buy the model for Raw Meat (Harry Kerslake), a crew mate who was having trouble finding a girl friend. With a pair of sun glasses, a lovely dress and a wig, she made a stunning entrance at Dolan's the dock-side pub now gone, where the thirstiest racers used to drink.

Even Russell Slade and Tryg Halvorsen, who for some reason were dancing on the bar, stopped and took notice. Russell, then a big shot at Bond's, insisted that Curly go back up the street to buy Delphine a pair of Cottontails, his company's famous under garment.

The joke went on and on: Delphine was kidnapped one night by the Navy cadets crewing for Peter Warner on Astor. A car chase to Dover to intercept Astor was successful and Delphine returned to Hobart just in time for the presentation of prizes in City Hall.

Curly and Mickleborough carried Delphine onto the stage and propped her on the grand piano. Secretary of the CYCA in those days Merv Davey, livid with rage, poked Delphine in the boobs and hissed: "Get that thing out of here." At which Delphine sat up and said: "Get your hands off me."

Dotty Sawyer from Melbourne, in Delphine's outfit, sunglasses and wig, had acted her part wonderfully, Merv got the shock of his life and the Lord Mayor's wife almost fell off her chair with laughter.

Curly, Mickleborough and the rest of the Ilina crowd were in deep trouble. But after suitable letters of apology and the passage of time, they were forgiven if not forgotten.

Curly, thanks. It was all worth it.

1987 America's Cup bomb scare

KOOKABURRA'S SKIPPER IAIN Murray did not have a lot to laugh about in the final match of the 1987 America's Cup as Stars & Stripes slid steadily from view but, sustained by a good-humoured bunch around him, he did manage to see the lighter side of hoax bomb threat:

"Our chase boat came alongside and said, 'You've got a bomb on board, what do you want to do?'

"We checked our option list. Our immediate response to them was, 'well what's the bad news?'

"Then we thought, 'Well this is our chance to find out what life's about after Twelve Metre racing.'

"And we took the third option, to continue with the race as we were well behind and we didn't think if the bomb went up that it was not going to affect the result.

"There was one other option. We could have appealed for average points."

Murray's inseperable companion Cliff ("the Wonder Dog") absolutely stole the show at the last press conference when he miraculously appeared and laid his head on Murray's shoulder just as Dennis Conner was telling Murray how he sympathised with him in losing the America's Cup:

"I know the way Iain is feeling right now and I would like to express to him and Kevin Parry what a terrific job you all did ..."

Conner got no further as the conference erupted in laughter at the appearance of Cliff. "I'm not trying to be funny," he said. Then he spotted Cliff, who never left

Cliff the dog upstages Iain Murray (centre) and Kevin Parry

Murray's side when he was ashore, putting his black and yellow head on his master's shoulder.

"Upstaged by a dog," laughed Conner. "And I thought I'd got rid of Liberty (Liberty was the Twelve in which Conner lost the Cup in 1983)."

Country road sailing

Two fun-loving Sydney Etchells sailors Mike Siddle and Paul Ramsay were driving a rental car down a flat, straight, country road in southern New South Wales when they ran out of petrol, miles from anywhere.

However, a stiff breeze was blowing from almost dead astern; just the right angle for a spinnaker. So they opened the car doors and sure enough, the vehicle began to roll slowly but steadily down the road.

Eventually they came across a fisherman with his trailer-boat parked on the side of the road. The courtesy of the sea prevailed and the fisherman gave them enough two-stroke outboard mix to shove in the parched fuel tank and get the car, sputtering a bit, onto the next town.

Blow into the bag

Bill Sweetapple, owner/skipper of the fast Farr 37 Pippin, would like to share around an experience he had with the good-natured Sydney Water Police at the start of the past season's Sydney-Hobart race:

"As Pippin rounded the sea mark in the 20-knot nor'easter the spinnaker was hoisted with such vigour that the clip fastening its bag to the rail was torn off and the bag fell overboard as we raced off at eight knots.

"Within minutes, the bow of the police launch Price appeared, perilously close to our port quarter. And as Sergeant Poole handed us back our bag, which his crew had retrieved, he said: "Blow into this.""

Buddha's free pass

Sad news for seafaring visitors to Port Lincoln is that Bevan ("Buddha") Woods and his wife Lindy have given up running the Lincoln hotel and have gone walkabout, by camper van, around Australia.

Buddha, who was an active crewman with the Port Lincoln YC's fleet, was a publican of amazing energy, good humour and tolerance who built the hotel into a thriving business that included an excellent bistro restaurant specialising in the port's famous seafood.

He once gave me a free pass, framed I guess in earlier times of the Lincoln's history, which read:

"This pass is good on all taxi cabs, railways and air routes provided that the bearer walks, carries his own luggage, swims all rivers and stops for drinks and smokes at the Lincoln Hotel.

"This pass is not transferable, except to another man with money."

The pass contains a collection of many other pieces of old-time pub lore, like: "A man is kept engaged in the yard to do all the cursing, swearing and bad language that is required in this establishment.

Buddha Woods and friend outside the Lincoln Hotel

"A dog is kept to do the biting. The undertaker calls every morning for orders."

Buddha may be gone, but I think I'll hang onto the pass as a memento of some fine times at the Lincoln.

Auscrew party, 1987

THIS COLUMN IS filed from Cowes, on the eve of the Champagne Mumm Admiral's Cup and hangovers are abounding in some quarters. For last night was the famous Auscrew party – usual place, Spencer's rigging loft, usual time, usual result, although there were some complaints that it was too quiet. The beer-throwing began a good two hours after the party started instead of the usual 40 minutes.

Auscrew, let me explain, is an organisation of sailors who are either British and have raced on Australian yachts or Australians who have raced on British yachts. It does much to promote friendship and hospitality among the offshore sailors of both countries.

During the evening, the Auscrew Award – an upside-down Australia on base – was presented to Kookaburra II's skipper Iain Murray for "screwing up the world's greatest regatta". Murray was in Cowes to race on Peter Kurts' Swan Premium III. All Australian team members were honoured guests at the party. Kurtsy, ever the forward planner, had the foresight to turn up in a German soldier's helmet.

The true currency of the award to Murray can best be described by the incident that led to first one being made, to Johnson Wooderson, a fun-loving and famous British yachtsman, in 1975.

Woody, steering Battlecry, shaved her close to the Royal Sovereign Light Tower; so close that when the yacht stood upright in the lee of the tower, the mast poked through an extended catwalk.

Battlecry, imprisoned by her mast on a falling tide was in danger of destruction against the tower's base. The crew took the only option left; let go the rigging, engage the engine and break the mast!

Battlecry went to her next start with fenders at the masthead and at the Auscrew party; Woody was presented with a battered Windex.

Winner of the award last Admiral's Cup was Australia's David Forbes, for spearing team yacht Drake's Prayer into a shipping buoy before the series began, necessitating a difficult and costly repair.

Murray was lucky to win this year from another contender, "Squashball" (real name Stuart Munro), brother of the famous British crewman "Rubber ball" (Alastair Munro).

Sailing on Jamarella in the British trials, Squashball ran back from the foredeck to get a wrench to free a jammed snap shackle. Hastening to return to the bow, he pushed his hands against the Kevlar genoa - and shot straight through it and overboard, leaving the outline of his corpulent frame as a neat hole in the sail.

Jamarella returned, retrieved him safely and still won the race.

Cricket in Rushcutters Bay

THE ADVENT OF the AWA Southern Cross Cup year (1987) means, besides a lot more visitors cluttering up the Darling Point Barbecue Club, the biennial Rest of the World versus Cruising Yacht Club of Australia cricket test (yachting division) in Rushcutters Bay Park, Sydney.

People tend to forget the scores (the CYCA has always won) but remember who won the man-of-the-match award. Past award winners have included Curley and Chas from Tas.

This year, says Knocker White, who is to be umpire, the match will be held on Monday, December 14. Curley will captain the CYCA and the Rest of the World will be captained by Tex.

Tex? He's a large American with a spiky haircut who turned up in Sydney some time last year and has stayed to toil on various boats.

Had he ever seen a cricket match? "Yeah, I've seen a bit of it on TV and frankly, I would rather check the air pressure in my tyres or go out to the airport and watch the planes take off.

"But I am looking forward to it, being my first time ... and being American, we always win."

Water fights

I'VE SEEN MORE strife through water fights in my time than any other manoeuvre, with possibly Laser starts and wing-mark roundings excepted.

There was the night in a Middle Harbour twilight for instance when we won the water fight but put a hole in a brand-new demonstration boat; not to mention the marital strife that ensues when the aprés-twilight clobber on the lady becomes saturated before she can savour the first g and t in the clubhouse.

However, the most notable recent water fight casualty is indeed the most notable, with some BIG names involved. Maybe they should not be named, but to protect the innocent, let's do it anyway.

The crew of Michael Coxon, Iain Murray and Steve Wheeler, tied Coxon's North Sydney Station on for the multiple tow home from the Manly Circle to Sydney Harbour well pleased with themselves after scoring two second placings in the first two heats of the NSW Etchells 22 championship.

So a water fight broke out. Amid the weaving around that went on, North Sydney Station broke free of the tow somehow and its stern was clipped by the next boat, Ramshackle.

Wheeler, trying to fend off, ended up shaken but okay on the bow of Ramshackle. That same bow clipped inside North Sydney Station's backstay to fold the mast, which had taken weeks to tune, neatly in half.

The Wetsundays

FUNNY, THE BROCHURES for the Whitsundays and for that matter, yachting magazine articles, never show pictures of rain bucketing down.

A friend, who is in the advertising business, went up there for a few days' relaxation with his wife.

After four days of solid rain, with reading material running out, the lady said: "According to this brochure there's a 50 per cent chance of sunny weather here this time of year."

Advertising man: "It's worse than you think. I wrote the brochure."

Monkey business

SAILMAKERS ARE USED to hearing all kinds of strange and wonderful excuses from their customers when they come in bearing torn sails for repair with "owner error" usually the real story.

But even the bullet-proof Peter Cowman of the Sobstad loft in Sydney had to sit down and laugh a bit when handed a spinnaker with a ragged hole in its centre with the explanation: "a monkey bit it."

Just before the AWA Sydney-Hobart race, John Hughes had laid the sail out in Rushcutters Bay Park when one of the denizens of that area came along with a pet monkey.

"Don't let your monkey run on my sail," said Hughes, "He might tear it."

"It's okay," said the monkey's owner. "His paws are smooth."

Whereupon the monkey, probably frustrated by not being able to join the discussion, chewed a hole in the sail.

Design fault

AN ENORMOUS SQUALL on Lake Macquarie flattened a mixed racing fleet. One yacht, designed by a well-known Lake identity being sailed by his sons, went to the bottom. Luckily, they were in shallow water and were able to cling to the top of the mast to await rescue.

Son on returning home that night: "Dad, if that mast had been four feet shorter, we would have drowned."

Father: "I knew there was something wrong with that boat when I designed it."

George Mottle's soup

NOSTALGIA AND LOTS of other things flowed freely when former crewmen of the Rooklyn racing team gathered to honour their owner-skipper Jack Rooklyn on the occasion of his 80th birthday in Sydney.

There were many good stories but the one I liked best concerned the culinary capabilities of my old friend and sometimes shipmate George Mottle - always a tower of strength in the galley but with a liking for hot additives that headed off any constipation problems.

The time was 1973, the place the English Channel, the boat Apollo on Jack's very first overseas campaign.

The one about George (related at the lunch by Peter Shipway) concerned the Cowes-Dinard race a couple of weeks beforehand.

The night was foul, with the wind blowing 35 knots, cold and wet, with waterproofs needed below as well as on deck and no-one feeling too sharp, let alone tackling the problem of preparing food.

George cheered everyone up by opening several cans of soup, which he poured into a big pot and began to heat and stir.

Shivering away on deck, Shipway and Greg Gilliam were driven crazy with anticipation by the aromas drifting from below. "I can't wait to get at that soup," said Shipway.

Finally George appeared in the companionway but no spoons or plates.

"Where are the utensils George?" Gilliam asked.

The reply was maddeningly delayed by George's famous stutter that is hard to reproduce in words, but went like this, "Hupmah ... hupmah ... throw this over the side, I have just been sick in it!"

George Mottle

Bowker married!

FRASER JOHNSON RETURNED from sailing in the SORC with, untypically, very little to say about the racing off the Florida coastline but with the outstanding news that Peter Bowker had got MARRIED!

Bowker, whose exploits as an itinerant navigator with mid-Atlantic nationality have often been chronicled in this column was, we all believed, an eternal bachelor. British-born Bowker sometime in the dim past gave up his job selling airline tickets because someone invited him to go on a long-distance yacht race. Since then, there has always been another yacht race.

The wedding to Josephine Van Der Sluit, was a quiet one in the garden of Bowker's house (another surprise) in Fort Lauderdale with Australian friend John ("The Fat Rabbit") Boulton best man.

But it did not end there. Bowker's friends got to hear about the quiet wedding, among them Ted Turner, with whom Bowker has sailed many miles. They gathered aboard the Bounty replica - the one Marlon Brando skippered in the 1960s movie, which Turner now owns - for a party.

They tied Bowker to the mast, flogged him and subjected him to various other indignities for deserting bachelordom after all those years.

Bowker confessed that getting married hadn't been as bad as going to the dentist. And he did get married on February 29, so has to buy an anniversary present only once every four years.

Batten vacuumed

REMEMBER THE MAYHEM - broken masts, ripped sails, one boat sunk when the 1988 world championship Etchells fleet was caught in a violent storm off Palm Beach, NSW?

Only recently I learned that Queensland competitor Noel Patterson had to get what was left of his top batten out of its pocket in the mainsail with a vacuum cleaner.

Jack Rooklyn and 'the sagos'

DON MICKLEBOROUGH AND I were recently talking over an experience I was fortunate enough to share aboard Jack Rooklyn's Ballyhoo in the Fastnet race of 1977.

We had battled all around the course in a light-air struggle against the Italian Il Moro di Venezia, which was ahead of us most of the way. When the crew took out their frustrations by referring to the Italians in derogatory terms like: "Where are those rotten .... (rhymes with sago) bastards? Jack would order them to stop: "They are fine sportsmen and worthy opponents. You are not to speak of them in that way."

Finally, in the last few miles to the finish, thanks to some inspired light air tactics and steering by and Greg Gilliam and Billy Peterson, we passed the Italians to take line honours.

Soon after we berthed, Jack went off to talk to the fine sportsmen on the worthy opponent Il Moro. Apparently it didn't go too well, because on his return, he fumed: "Those rotten .... (rhymes with sago) bastards wouldn't have anything to do with me!"

J trawled

DURING A CLUB race on Sydney Harbour in September 1988, a 50kt squall flattened the J24 fleet. One of them, Jay, a boat that had yielded as much fun as well as some good racing to a group headed by Ralph Gudjerhan and had certainly broached many times before, this time was virtually driven under by the force of the wind.

Water poured into the companionway and swamped her. She sank while under tow near Bradley's Head leaving the crew rescued and safe but shocked and boatless.

Attempts to locate Jay were fruitless and eventually the insurance company paid out on her as a total loss. Ralph I understand, disillusioned with sailing, went off and bought a motor cruiser, his crew dispersed to other classes.

Then on January 27 the following year, a prawn trawler snagged its nets on an object near Bradley's Head and the Maritime Services Board raised from the bottom the obstruction that proved to be Jay.

The hull and mast were intact, just covered with growth. The major damage was to stanchions down one side and the pulpit, suggesting that the boat had speared sideways into the harbour bed and probably stuck there.

Marine insurance assessor John Messenger believes the huge spectator fleet on Australia Day for the ANZ 12 Metre Challenge disturbed the waters of the harbour so vigorously that Jay popped up from the mud, awaiting the first prawn trawler's net.

Jay after four months on the bottom of Sydney Harbour

The good news was that jewellery valued at more than $2000 was recovered intact from the cabin. And the 5hp outboard stowed on the cabin sole, after a hose-out with fresh water, fuel drained and replaced, started and ran perfectly.

Subsequently

sailmaker Ian MacDiarmid, his offsider John Hearn and J24 sailor Alex Nemeth bought the remains from the insurance company that had already paid out on the boat as a total loss.

They changed the name to Bottom of the Harbour.

Fearless Fred

I'D HEARD FROM Ted Kaufman, who skippered Mercedes III in Australia's 1967 Admiral's Cup win, that one of his crewmen, Fred Thomas, had been seriously ill.

Fearless Fred, as we all knew him, had some time before dropped out of offshore racing and the Sydney scene and moved to the Gold Coast, where he does some rigging and sails recreationally on his own sweet little yacht.

A few weeks later, hanging around for XXXX/Ansett Hamilton Island Race Week, a holler from the group sitting on the rock wall outside the Barefoot Bar alerted me to the presence of Fearless Fred. Fearless indeed he had turned out to be, as he described the horrendous treatment that had given him remission from a rare form of cancer.

With him was another former leading player in the Australian ocean racing scene, Graham Shields, founder of sparmaker Alspar and one of the world's most innovative spar designers. The pair of them were cruising the Whitsundays aboard Graham's Nantucket 38 Caledonian.

They invited me aboard for a beer the following day and I took along Fraser Johnson, who knew them both and had also sailed with Ted Kaufman for an exchange of experiences.

"Ted sacked me twice from his crew," said Fred. "But we have remained good friends."

Fraser and I were impressed by the range of imported beers on Caledonian. I was just finishing off a Becks when Graham informed me that it was home brew. "The brewery is in the aft cabin, have a look."

Sure enough, there was a neat little piece of apparatus, giving an occasional burble, cooking up the brown stuff from a Coopers home brew pack.

A boat with its own brewery is certainly a first in my experience and representing an advance among serious cruising mode people comparable with the winged keel and perhaps the introduction of sliced bread and canned beer.

Fred and Graham were collecting the stack of exotic-labelled designer beer bottles I had noticed on the dock alongside the boat from bars along the coast and were heading for Shaw Island where Graham had noticed a little stream coming down a hill that promised excellent water for the next brew.

So after sinking a few, discussing the problems of ocean racing in general ("It was at its peak in the days of the Halvorsens and the Swansons when people really knew how to sail ... Gordon Ingate did more for the sport than anyone really appreciates ... the races to Coogee and back were better than the present-day triangles because you never knew what wind conditions and angles to expect" – Fred's views), Fraser and I rose to leave.

"Let me give you my card so when you are up the coast you can look me up," said Fred.

As we pocketed a card each for "Fred's Rigging", he added, "That will be 17 cents; that's what it cost me to have each one printed."

I found 20 cents and invited Fred, who is on an invalid pension, to keep the change. Fraser, who had just stepped ashore from Beyond Thunderdome after a race had no money on him but handed Fred a packet of dental floss, which Fred accepted.

And we said goodbye for a while to a pair of yachting's great individuals that few of the new-generation sailors among the several hundred on the marina for Race Week would have had the pleasure of knowing.

Stripey on crocodile pies

CROCODILE PIES WERE among the delights offered during Race Week 1989 from the Hamilton Island bakery, one of the best anywhere run by a lady called Barbara who has imagination as well as a great way with tucker.

I tried to buy one for our very own Queensland correspondent Ian ("Stripey") Grant who declined, saying he had an understanding with crocodiles: "I don't bite crocodiles and they don't bite me!"

Ian ('Stripey') Grant

Sprouley's rats

DAVID SPROULE, THE manic photographer from The Australian, had a few of us rolling on the floor at Hamilton Island one night as he was extolling the virtues of rats as pets.

He has had three: Hamish, Rastus and Rodney. "They are intelligent, emotional, affectionate," said Sprouley, who has a little yacht he sails around Moreton Bay. "And they make excellent depth sounders. If they try to jump overboard, you know it's time to tack to miss the mud."

His first pair of rats, Hamish and Rastus, suffered fates that would bring a tear to a glass eye. Rastus was trapped by a storm in the back yard and drowned. Hamish somersaulted off the balcony of the home unit.

But his current rat, Rodney, has settled well in his new home, which happens to be a budgie cage because the previous pair was given to chewing bits out of the houses Sprouley built for them from expensive marine plywood.

Sprouley is concerned, however, that the habitat may be causing a personality change in Rodney, who has taken to sitting on the swing and in other ways starting to act like a budgie. "He looks like a budgie in a fur coat," said Sproule.

Southerly's beer bust

ON THE OCCASION of Southerly's win in the annual veterans' race staged by the Cruising Yacht Club of Australia in 1989, satisfied owner Don Mickleborough related one of the many yarns about his 50-year-old boat, a 35ft Charlie Peel design built in Huon pine.

He recalled the passage from Hobart to Auckland, after the Sydney-Hobart race, to contest the 1961 Auckland-Sydney transTasman race. The vivid part of the memory was being caught in a cyclone off Cape Reinga at the north-western tip of New Zealand's North Island.

Southerly was in cyclonic conditions for two and a-half days. The wind peaked at 89 knots and with current running against the wind at five to six knots, the waves were fearsome.

Southerly, down to storm jib and with the main rolled in to leave only 8ft of luff hoisted, fell hard off two waves. As she hit after dropping off the second, there was a heart-rending crash when 10 dozen of the 24 dozen bottles of beer stowed in the bilge shattered. And they were the BIG bottles that were then standard.

Don Mickleborough on Southerly, "The Great Floating Hotel", where there are no drinks before five.

Dougie Lintern quickly ripped up the floorboards and checked around for damage. The impact had sprung a plank quarter of an inch out of alignment and fractured a 3in square floor, so the situation was reasonably serious.

But Lintern came on deck laughing so hard that there were suspicions he had glass in his tongue from the now-potent bilge water. He explained: "You know those ten dozen cans Bert Dolan sold us in Hobart to try (cans were still a novelty at that time.)? Well, they are extra large ones. So we've still got about as much beer as we thought we had to start with."

Catalina sinker

FRANK HAMMOND, THE Melbourne sailmaker, was mentioned during the announcement at Royal Sydney Yacht Squadron, of the shift by Catalina Yachts from Melbourne to Sydney, as one of the few people ever to sink a Catalina; a feat that apparently earned him much respect during a tour of the Catalina Yachts factory in California.

Frank, who has been involved in more than one shipwreck, admitted the deed and explained: He was steering a Catalina 22, which is a trailerable yacht, in a race on Port Albert when she was caught by a severe squall on a lee shore.

The boat could not be tacked. The only solution was to gybe around to get on the leg towards deeper water. The keel had to be raised to allow the manoeuvre in shallowing water but after the gybe, it could not be lowered again quickly enough to stop the boat blowing over and swamping.

"I really knew it was going under as I felt the masthead light slipping through my feet," said Hammond.

On another occasion, he was ripping along in the middle of the night on Port Phillip Bay in a J24 in which he shared ownership. Suddenly the boat hit a reef with a tremendous crash and bounced off, waking Hammond's partner in the boat who had been sleeping below.

The partner emerged from the hatchway, rubbed his eyes and said: "Hammond, remind never to lend you my car," and went back to sleep.

Lord Lichfield's upgrade

THE EARL OF Lichfield, Patrick Lichfield, that superb creative photographer best known for his photographs of the Royal Family, brushed with international yachting at the 1987 America's Cup in Fremantle and as official photographer aboard Rothmans on the Fremantle to Auckland leg of the 1989-90 Whitbread around-the-world race.

Lord Lichfield's work keeps him travelling steadily and during a visit to Sydney in 1989 and at a small dinner party for media types put together by Rothmans he asked me, of all people, for a bit of local knowledge about the Fremantle-Auckland run and advice in general on being at sea in a yacht.

Short of telling him to take plenty of Vitamin E cream for gunwale bum and then having to explain what that was; giving him the wishful thinking for the leg (hard downwind run all the way under spinnaker) there wasn't much I could tell him.

So to divert the conversation from my lack of worthwhile knowledge, I asked him if he had done much sailing. "No, but my ancestor, Admiral Lord Anson did," he said. It turned out that in the 18th century Lord Anson circumnavigated the globe in a voyage lasting three years and nine months.

He may be short on yachting knowledge but Lord Lichfield has been a keen student of life in general and he warmed up the proceedings by stating that he enjoyed the company of drunken old journalists (which explained why I had been invited in the first place).

During his earlier years, working for an agency on Fleet Street, he told us, he was assigned for a job in the Caribbean with a well-known writer who was also a well-known soak. He tried to introduce himself to the man, who was supporting himself heavily against the bar at Heathrow Airport and who waved him aside with, "Can't talk now; I've got to fly out with some twit called Lichfield."

Lord Patrick Litchfield, at the Rothmans Sydney dinner party

Introductions eventually made the young Lord Lichfield helped the writer through the touch-and-go situation of whether he was sober enough to fly at all, onto the plane. Mercifully, the soak subsided quickly into slumber alongside him.

Sometime later, Lord Lichfield returned from a visit to the lavatory to find his companion's seat (in economy) empty. Concerned, when a stroll around the plane revealed no sight of the writer, he sought help from a cabin attendant.

"Don't worry, sir," said the attendant. "While you were away Lord Lichfield made himself known to us and we have shifted him to first class."

'Big Kite's' negotiation

DURING THE BIG Kite Ball fund-raiser for leukemia research in memory of David ("Big Kite") Stephens, who bravely resisted the dreaded disease for one last season of fabulous sailing on 18-footers, the story was related of Big Kite becoming so angry after an argument with skipper Peter Sorensen that he jumped off the boat before it reached the Sydney Flying Squadron ramp and swam ashore.

He left Sorensen and crewman Andrew Buckland on the capsized boat and unable to carry get it out of the water without him. So they bargained in beer before Kite would help them.

Buckland, confirming the story, added: "We had a really bad day on the water ending with a complete misunderstanding between Kite and Sorro (who

Big Kite Stephens racing forward with Andrew Buckland Peter Sorensen

is a bit deaf).

"On the sail in after the race, the argument just got worse and worse. It ended up with Sorro trying to beat Big Kite on the back with the tiller extension.

"So yes, Kite did jump off and swim ashore in Careening Cove and yes, we could not get the boat out without him and it all continued with Kite on shore and Sorro promising him an ever-increasing supply of beer to return.

"The final terms of settlement were that Sorro buy beer for Big Kite and all his mates, all night!"

Nick is not dead

IT IS MY pleasant duty to resurrect an old shipmate, Nick Kosalov, put away by the editor of this journal in his column.

Firstly, Nick was listed as "among those who have sailed their last voyage" in the annual report of the Cruising Yacht Club of Australia. Then, at the Quiet Little Drink dinner reunion of Hobart racers, Nick was among those remembered with two minutes' silence.

So the editor wrote Nick into a glutinous piece about the fraternity of ocean racing. A few weeks later Tony Cable, who presides at the QLD, cornered the editor in the CYCA bar and said: "I've got some good news and some bad news. I enjoyed your piece but Nick is not dead.

"Boy Messenger had a beer with him two weeks ago"

Nick Kosalov

How come? It seems that correspondence from the club to Nick down in Cooma or some place near there kept coming back until someone in the system, through frustration, pencilled "deceased" on the envelope. To paraphrase Mark Twain, reports of Nick's death were grossly exaggerated.

Boat names

ANOTHER PINCH FROM Troppo News, the entertaining journal of the Cairns Yacht Club: One boat owner we know has named his boat The Missus and the Kids so that he can say he is not out sailing enjoying himself but doing the right thing with his wife and children.

Another had a boat called The Office; that he went to too often. And yet another named his boat After You and that's what he tells his missus: "I named the boat after you."

Our own household has been going through the throes of trying to select the name for a new boat with likely entries chalked on the message board in the kitchen. Only trouble with that arrangement is the boat is likely to end up being called "Eye Doctor Tuesday" or "Get Mushrooms and Onions".

Boat bag cleaned up

THE ENTHUSIASM OF the waterfront volunteers in the very worthy Clean up Australia Day, inspired by yachtsman Ian Kiernan, netted from Port Jackson another fine haul of syringes, plastics, polystyrene, abandoned cars and other odds and ends – and more.

It seems that volunteers in a dinghy descended with glad cries on this huge piece of blue plastic they found floating in Middle Harbour. They had a bit of trouble for a while. It was tangled by some sort of rope arrangement to a nearby mooring buoy.

So they cut it free, towed it ashore and proceeded to hack into readily disposable pieces a protective boat bag awaiting the absent boat, valued by its owner at about $500.

'Raw Meat' remembered

GEORGE PEARCE, KNOWN sometimes as "Raw Meat", brother of Sydney sailmaker Joe Pearce and for many years one of Joe's and later Hood Sailmakers' valued workers renowned for strong and neat workmanship on those all-important corners of sails and finishing work, passed away in 1990.

George, who was brought up in Woolloomooloo in its hard days, was also one of the top crewmen in the early post World War Two years of ocean racing. He sailed aboard leading yachts of that time like the Livingston brothers' Kurrewas and young Rupert Murdoch's Ilina.

Mostly, Raw was part of a threesome with "Thunder" (Harry Kerslake) and "Earrings" (John Love). They were inseparable and formidable ashore as well as afloat.

A big gathering of sailing friends turned out for George's funeral. Clean up Australia campaigner Ian Kiernan spoke at the service in a moving but simple way about George and later had more to say in the column he writes for Sydney Afloat.

The column was headed: "Raw Meat joins Thunder and Earrings". It began: On Sunday 17th May I was enjoying the fresh southwest breeze on the harbour when it freshened to a blustery 25 knots and I ducked behind Middle Head to reef and set the old bullet proof number two jib that Raw Meat had made 20 years earlier. I tacked up the harbour looking at the sail and thinking what a great craftsman Raw was.

"Monday morning I received a call to say that George had quietly slipped his mooring lines and gone to join his brother Joe and old mates Thunder and Earrings at some endless regatta in the sky."

Only problem with that moving piece was – Earrings was able to read it. He is alive and well and was in the front row of the funeral service addressed by Kiernan.

Kiernan, the editor of Sydney Afloat Robin Copeland and some old sailing friends, took Earrings to lunch at the CYCA a week or so later to square things away. He is well and enjoying a quiet life close to home in Surry Hills, far removed from his more hectic days on the waterfront.

The rest of Kiernan's tribute to George Pearce was beautifully put: "His passing probably represents the end of an era. Through that time he has shown us a simple love for the harbour, boats, things maritime and his mates.

"His casual but sound advice, his slow smile, his humour and encouragement to young sailors, certainly left us richer and wiser for his being, you might say, not bad for an old sailmaker."

The story I like best about the playful side of George Pearce was told to me by Tony Cable, a ship-mate of George's in a time-distant Hobart race. As the weather got colder going south, Raw kept adding layers of clothing so by the time he got to Hobart, he smelt a bit.

Nothing too novel about that – it's a practice followed by just about everyone these days and the state of arrival in terms of aroma is common to all.

But George, apparently, was tardy about heading for the showers and so defiant when some of his crew mates pushed him under the hot water that he calmly ate the soap.

'armless tattoo

PHIL ("BEAR") THOMPSON the yard and marina superintendent at the Cruising Yacht Club of Australia, for 15 years battled a type of bone cancer with a heroism that did not allow him to dwell upon it – at least, in the company of other people.

Finally, however, with the exhaustion of all other medical remedies, Phil had to face the grim prospect of having the arm amputated, along with most of the shoulder.

A day or so before he was due to go in into hospital for the operation, a few of his mates – including those who sailed with him on Challenge II when she won the IMS division of the 1989 Sydney-Hobart race – decided the arm should have a wake.

Phil was in good spirits after a few quiet beers down at Rushcutters Bay and so were his mates. They all decided it would be a good idea to take Phil up to Kings Cross and have the arm tattooed.

The tattooist made a marvellous job of the barquentine in full sail and was pleased with his work until The Bear's supporters began haggling about price and whether the tattoo was guaranteed to stay on.

"No, you can't have a discount and yes, it won't come off," the tattooist said.

About then, Phil's minders dropped the word that the whole arm was coming off the following day.

I gather that a bench-load of tough looking bikies, waiting for their turn with the tattooist, went collectively pale.

Later, hospital staff were gratified that they were removing a tattoo. Phil made a good recovery. Framed on the wall at his home is a picture of the tattoo, lightning sketched on the night by Peter McAdam, one of his crew-mates from Challenge II.

When Kay Cottee left the iron on

KAY COTTEE, THE first woman to sail single-handed around the world, non-stop and unassisted, isn't all that keen on racing. She would have someone else steer her yacht, the now-famous Blackmore's First Lady, when she contested the twilight races on Pittwater.

One evening, however, that someone else was not available and she had to drive the boat herself. Her pre-start manoeuvring was so cautions that the rest of the fleet took off and in not much wind, finally drifted across the line after everyone else.

A male voice boomed from the start boat; "Did you leave the iron on, love?"

"I have not raced since and I am sure he had a hand in making me take off around the world," Kay said.

'Rubber Ball's response

GENIAL POMMIE YACHTING journalist friend Bob Fisher, who trained as a thespian in his youth and later worked for BBC radio and television before becoming a freelance writer/photographer, was technical advisor to the now-concluded British yachting soap (what a contradiction in terms) Howard's Way

He somehow managed to get himself a yacht out of the deal, the 45ft light-displacement Barracuda, which featured in the show and which Fisher races keenly when in residence at his house near Lymington on The Solent.

Sometimes Alastair ("Rubber Ball") Munro sails with him. Rubber Ball, so named because of his shape, is among the best British offshore sailors and one of the funniest; in dry wit terms, at least.

Fisher told me of the time he put a lovely new spinnaker, straight from the sailmaker, aboard the boat. It had that wonderful fresh fragrance and the tag ends of thread that fell out of it as it went up for the first time indicated that it was indeed straight from the loft floor.

Then came the call from the foredeck for "stickyback" from the sail repair kit. "You bastards haven't torn it already?" Fisher bellowed.

Retorted Rubber Ball: "Well, you can't expect these things to last forever."

On another occasion, Barracuda was hammering along some place in the middle of the night when a squall flattened her. It was one of those lovely British summer evenings – cold, windy, driving rain – but Fisher dived out of his bunk and clad in nothing more than his jocks heroically headed for the mast and began fumbling with the reefing lines.

He was still struggling about there a couple of minutes later when Rubber Ball, who had the good sense to drag on some warm gear and waterproofs, appeared at his side and said: "Do you have change of a fiver?"

A chastened Fisher stepped aside and Rubber Ball proceeded to tackle the job efficiently and rapidly.

Seasick cures continued

THE STORY OF the conversation a very seasick Nick Feros had in the 1990 Hobart race with his partner in the ownership of Bobsled, Geoff Bush, varies with the telling.

Feros either offered to sell his half of the boat to Bush for $150 provided he could immediately get off it, or Feros offered Bush his half share and $150 for the same deal.

There is, however, an addendum: Feros, tethered by his harness and lying in the bottom of the cockpit, was welcoming the waves that regularly washed over him. "They're lovely and warm ... when the next wave comes, please cut my harness and let me go with it."

Bobsled achieved speeds in Bass Strait, up to 26.8 knots, that would blow your pants off, literally. Ask Gary ("Buck") Johnston. During a change from mainsail to storm trysail, Buck washed overboard as he was down to leeward, lashing the mainsail to the boom.

Secured by his safety harness to the boat, he was still in trouble as no-one had noticed his plight. "I was going down for about the fifth mouthful," he said. "I guess I was in the water for about 30 seconds before someone noticed my legs trailing out from under the boom and grabbed me."

By the time he regained the deck, his pants were gone and his jocks were around his knees.

Vic Meyer, swimming coach

VIC MEYER, ONE of the toughest and most successful ocean-racers of the 1950s and 1960s, died at his home in Buderim, on Queensland's Sunshine Coast, in May 1991.

Meyer, an engineer, was born in Switzerland. He came to Australia at the age of 19 after a short trial period as a gaucho (cowboy) on the pampas of Argentina. After building a successful business and trying out sports such as skiing and ice skating, he took up firstly motor boating and then sailing.

He made his motor cruiser Lauriana available to the Cruising Yacht Club of Australia as radio relay vessel for the 1952 Sydney-Hobart race and announced afterwards: "I will not follow the race; I will be in it."

He commissioned Alan Payne to design the 57ft yawl Solo, which he built in steel at his own iron foundry in Sydney. He launched her in June 1954 and won five out of eight races before Christmas that year, despite his lack of ocean-racing experience.

Over the next six years Solo became the most successful ocean racer of her time with corrected time wins in the 1956 and 1962 Sydney-Hobart races and line honours wins in the 1958 and 1959 Sydney-Hobarts.

Meyer quickly learned all the skills of yacht racing until there was nothing he could not do on Solo better than anyone else, although he would never take the helm during a race. He was forever working on Solo, re-siting fittings with his oxy welder, striving to improve the boat.

He was one of the first hard-driving Australian skippers to follow the spinnaker-carrying philosophy: "Leave it on until it blows out and then put up another one." He was a tough skipper to sail for and went through crews very quickly, although anyone who sailed with him learned from the experience.

Another tough man of the time Syd Brown, the Auckland fisherman, told a great story of one Hobart start where Vic gave him the helm and said, "Steer straight for the Heads

From left: Syd Brown, Len Burke and Butch Dalrymple-Smith

and don't alter course for anything."

Syd recalled: "It was a strong southerly and I couldn't see a thing for the spinnaker. We ran clean over a dinghy full of Greek fishermen off Shark Island. One of them was cursing Vic from the water yelling, 'You basta, I cannot swim.' "Vic waved his arms over his head freestyle fashion and yelled back, 'Quick, go like this!'"

America's Cup campaigning, San Diego
REMEMBER BACK TO the 1987 America's Cup campaign when Syd Fischer, to gather support for his challenge from his home city, called his yacht Steak 'n' Kidney (rhyming slang for Sydney)?

The memories of that campaign are hazier in the USA and rhyming slang little known although Graham ("Frizzle") Freeman, the renowned Tasmanian over there working as dock master for the Italian Il Moro di Venezia team, is doing his best to spread the word and puzzling the Italians no end with it.

And so the San Diego Tribune, in reporting a press conference with Iain Murray, said: "Murray's syndicate is not the only one representing Australia. Syd Fischer who owns Steak and Kidney, a chain of Australian restaurants, is also mounting a one-boat campaign."

"Bloody typical of these Yank papers," observed an Australian friend of mine living in Los Angeles, when I showed her the report. She is a crossword buff who enjoys tackling the big one in the Los Angeles Times.

One day she swooped on the clue, "Native of Australia" with a glad cry of recognition but was totally unable to make "aborigine" fit the spaces and in frustration had to wait for the answer in the following day's paper.

And the answer was: "Maori".

Sir Robbo names a boat
BOB ROBERTSON, THE self-proclaimed "Sir Robbo of Queensland", as well as being one of the state's best offshore campaigners, builds production yachts and had recently launched a fine new design by the young Seaflyer design team David Lyons and Tony Laubraux, the Robertson 950.

Sir Robbo is not one of your quiet achievers. After a race he soon lets everyone know forcefully of his triumphs and even his disasters.

Sir Robbo of Queensland at the helm

The first yacht out of the moulds has been called Corrobboree, with the emphasis on the "robbo".

With the design notes is supplied a dictionary definition of corrobboree: "n. 1. Aboriginal assembly of sacred, festive or warlike characters. 2. Any large or noisy gathering. 3. A disturbance; an uproar."

3, I think, best fits Sir Robbo.

Mark Foy's no tacking rule

A BOOKLET BY the founder of the Sydney Flying Squadron Mark Foy, published as a souvenir on the club's 50th anniversary, showed that Foy's ideas were radical indeed for their time and elements of them are still to be seen in 18-footer racing:

All boats shall have coloured sails with every alternate cloth being dyed some bright colour. The boats shall receive their handicaps at the start of the race under the Mark Foy system: first past the post to win the race except in the case of an upheld protest. The boats must always finish before the wind with everything set.

But there is another lesser-known rule in the booklet that makes you wonder if Mark Foy knew much about sailing: "The boats must not tack except for some unavoidable reason happening.

"They must, if necessary, sail beyond the buoy so that their course can be laid to their second buoy in a straight line.

"Boats by this arrangement go round the course as racehorses – or as all other running courses do – NO TACKING – it seems stupid to inexperienced people and they get puzzled and don't bother coming again to sailing races and you lose your supporters. They should easily see which boat is leading ALL the time.

"The boats must not force each other round onto the other tack; each must have a clear run to buoy, overtaking boats that cannot get to windward of the boat ahead without collision MUST go to leeward."

It is not clear whether this rule was ever implemented.

Rolls Royces all round

RYOUJI YODA, OWNER of the Japanese 50-footer Will, is a man with a sense of fun and in Cowes for the 1991 Admiral's Cup, he gave the best party of the regatta and must have impressed the right people because he was invited to dinner at the Royal Yacht Squadron.

As a result, perhaps, he became carried away by all things British. When Will rounded Fastnet Rock in second place, but 40 miles behind the French yacht Corum Saphir in the Fastnet race, he decided it was incentive time and told his crew: "If we beat Corum Saphir, I will buy each of you a Rolls Royce."

At the next position sked, Will's navigator was heard to say to the navigator on Corum Saphir: "If you let us beat you, we'll give you three Rolls Royces.

The French must have thought about it. They beat Will to the finish in Plymouth by only 19 minutes."

What's in a name?

I ONCE OWNED a Finn called Harvey Wallbanger and so loved the name of the outright winner of the 1991 Hervey Bay race for trailables: the Hartley 16 Hartley Wharfbanger.

Boy Messenger's biggest punt

AMONG HIS MANY other attributes, including skill on the water and at the pool table, E.C. ("Boy") Messenger is a good judge of horseflesh and has an incredibly accurate memory.

Back in 1949, when he was 25, he and some of his young mates persuaded his father Ernie Messenger to allow them to take his Independence in the Sydney-Hobart race.

She was a low-wooded 38-footer built in 1938 of kauri planking by Ernie Digby in Melbourne. Ernie Messenger bought her in 1949 and transported her by truck to Sydney. She had a new mainsail, bought from Harry West for 250 pounds, but campaigning funds were needed as Ernie had spent his budget for the boat on the mainsail.

"In those days you could go to Hobart for a hundred pounds," Messenger said in a group recollection at the bar of the Cruising Yacht Club of Australia as the 1991 Hobart race was coming around.

But that sort of money was still big for the times for the five young men crewing the boat. So each put in five pounds and sat around the telephone in the Messenger boatshed one Saturday while Boy worked his magic with an SP bookmaker.

One of the crew, Hamish Grieve, said: "Boy picked the local program except one and we had 80 pounds. And then he picked

Boy Messenger at the helm and Hamish Grieve

the winner in the last race at Flemington at nine to two. So we had 140 pounds and we went to Hobart."

Messenger added: "The horse was Chanak, in the Yan Yean Stakes, ridden by W. Williams and carrying eight stone six."

Independence, fourth into Hobart, set off on the return journey with 10 dozen bottles of Cascade, very valuable cargo in those beer-shortage ridden days and good for bartering up crayfish from fishermen along the way.

The boat had no motor and off Jervis Bay ran into gales that twice forced her back into port. That sent the whole crew broke so they spread the word at Malcolm's Cafe, a popular local hangout, that they had beer for sale.

"We had 50 people queued up on the dock in the morning and we sold them the beer for five bob a bottle. It ran out with 30 people still on the wharf," Messenger said.

Independence set out again into a 30-knot easterly which eventually became 80 knots, forcing the crew to heave to. With the yacht overdue, Ernie Messenger organised a search plane.

"The next door neighbour told him not to worry. 'Boy will be home by Saturday; the races are on at Randwick'", said Boy.

"On Friday afternoon we were off Jibbon and we passed some fishermen a couple of bottles of beer we just happened to have left and asked them to ring my father.

"We got through the Heads at 1am – to an enormous welcome. Dad came out with a ferry load of people. But the first thing he did when we berthed was to go round the boat in a dinghy.

"'Not one plank sprung!' he was able to proclaim proudly."

San Diego's sleaziest bar

I KNEW IT was my kind of place from the moment I walked in there and my companion ordered a vodka tonic with a twist of lime:

Jerry the bartender leaned forward and said firmly: "Lady, this is a dump! We serve only beer or wine."

The Kansas City Barbeque claimed proudly to be "San Diego's sleaziest bar". It was an anachronism in the downtown area, a tiny three-room shack sandwiched between the gleaming new hotel and office spires and ritzy waterfront restaurants of the marina district, where we stayed during the 1992 America's Cup.

The bar was dim, festooned with discarded brassieres, sailors' hats, yellowing pictures and posters from old movies and various other memorabilia including items from the America's Cup syndicates and attendant media team, which made it an approved watering hole.

But the food was good, it had more than 20 imported beers as well as the local draught, the service friendly and the place was always packed. It had been that way since it featured in the movie Top Gun.

The Top Gun production team, barman Jerry Grandquist told me, was driving past one day, looking at locations for the movie starring Tom Cruise and Kelly McGillis, when it picked up the delicious aroma of spare ribs barbecuing away and stopped for lunch.

Some ribs and ten pitchers of beer later, they decided this was to be the place for the sleazy bar scene which ends the movie about San Diego's navy pilots.

The movie made the modest establishment famous and sought out by tourist visitors. It does have more going for it. For six years running it was selected as the best barbecue restaurant in Southern California by San Diego magazine.

The proprietors cleverly neutralised its one major drawback, its proximity by only a metre or so from the tracks that carry enormously long freight trains right through San Diego's downtown area. When a train is rattling past, the whole place shakes and conversation is even more difficult than usual.

So they placed a sign in the bar which said:

"To commemorate those great trains that run all night across the USA, Kansas City Barbeque proudly serves Night Train – $1 a shot and only 25c a shot when a train passes by after 5pm. Imported all the way from Chula Vista, California."

As a train approaches, the barman hollers, "Night train" and the customers order up; sometimes by the tray load.

The offer is not as generous as the sign suggests. Says Jerry: "This stuff is called Cuervo Red but it fact it's rot gut. It's fortified apple wine, 19 per cent alcohol.

"It's probably the worst wine in America. For the last seven years the street people in New York have nominated this as their favourite drink.

"But we go through 15 cases a week. The Germans and the Austrians love it and the Japanese buy it by the case."

SINS 20th anniversary, 1992

THE 20TH ANNIVERSARY of the foundation of SINS (the Society of International Nautical Scribes) was marked by a special celebration in San Diego where many of its members were gathered for the 1992 America's Cup.

SINS began in Sydney in 1972 when a group of visiting and local journalists, frustrated by the lack of information and press facilities at the One Ton Cup, decided they needed an organisation to lobby the Cruising Yacht Club of Australia, the regatta organiser, for a better deal.

The first meeting was held on an extremely hot day in the children's wading pool at the Travelodge in Rushcutters Bay where some of the visitors were staying. A cooler of iced beer facilitated the discussions.

Twenty years on, after periods of high organisation punctuated by absolute chaos, SINS lives on, playing a somnolent role in union terms until an issue arises, but as a useful network of contacts worldwide and as an organiser of memorable parties at major regattas.

Bob Fisher, one of the British legends of the very first meeting, after a preliminary SINS party in San Diego, was having one of his usual high-decibel debates with an Australian co-founder over dinner, when he fell asleep at the restaurant table.

San Diego Sinners Bob Fisher (right), on the laptop and Stuart Alexander working on the sun tan

The group, with the help of a waiter whose sense of humour was sharpened by a five-dollar bill, moved quietly to a distant table, leaving the Pom snoring gently; the subject of photography and comment from other diners as they finished their meals and left for home.

The waiter was in the process of fabricating a bill for $2000 to leave with the sleeping Sinner when, unfortunately, he woke, stood up, straightened the yachting jacket and tie and left, with total dignity.

Buddy Melges one-liners

Buddy Melges, the 62-year-old skipper of Bill Koch's America 3 in the 1992 America's Cup win over Raoul Gardini's Il Moro di Venezia, skippered by Paul Cayard, showed again his mastery of the one-liners at the post-race press conferences in San Diego. Here are some examples:

On breakdowns: "The Hercules rocket people built Jayhawk, our first boat. Apparently they weren't aware the boat didn't go out just once – it had to make it back every night too."

On crew changes: "Someone asked me if we were having trouble making decisions. I immediately answered, 'Yes and no.'"

Noting that his wife Gloria is commodore of their local yacht club at Zenda, Wisconsin: "Not everybody can sleep with the commodore and admit it next day."

On carbon-fibre construction: "I remember when they built boats with tools. Now you build 'em with paint brushes."

On espionage: "Yeah we have it. We have this popcorn machine-looking thing on the front of one of the chase boats. It drives Cayard up the wall every time we point it at him."

On Zenda: "It's not the end of the world but you can see it from there."

When Boy ate Billy's dinner

THE PROGRESSION OF skiff sailors into keelboat classes and clubs is quite natural these days but 20 to 30 years ago the appearance of a "skiffie" in an august yacht club like the Royal Sydney Yacht Squadron was rare.

Two of the very first skiff sailors to race with the Squadron in the Dragon class were Billy Barnett and Boy Messenger. Barnett, besides having the respect of the whole fleet as the high-quality builder of Dragons, was a strong competitor. His win in a NSW championship came as no surprise.

There was a surprise, though, for Boy Messenger when he turned up at the Squadron to lodge his declaration after the last race. The then secretary of the RSYS and the Australian Yachting Federation, Lloyd Burgess, greeted him with great warmth.

"Join us for dinner," said Burgess.

Boy, slightly puzzled but never one to knock back a freebie, sat down in the dining room with the race officials as Burgess introduced him:

"Gentlemen, meet Mr Bill Barnett, our new state champion."

Boy, who is of similar wiry build to Barnett, in retelling the story added: "Billy has never forgiven me for eating his dinner."

How Stripey got his name

AUSTRALIAN SAILING MAGAZINE'S Queensland correspondent is known on both sides of the Tweed as "Stripey". In Southport I found out how he got his nickname.

When sailing was getting going again at the end of World War Two, he was selected as bailer-boy on a four-handed 12ft skiff going to Sydney for a carnival. He weighed just four stone seven pounds, used to chuck out the water with a baking dish and with agility dodge the flying feet through tacks.

Those were the days of clothing rationing; material of any kind was in short supply. For the trip south, his mum knocked him up a blazer made from pyjama material. He tells me it set a bit of a trend and the name it gave him, "Stripey Pyjamas" – soon shortened to "Stripey" – remained with him.

Clem's stew

CLEM MASTERS, BESIDES being a legendary designer, boatbuilder, navigator and sailor, was also a good sea cook (although it helped a lot if you were not overly worried about cholesterol). He sailed many ocean miles with Sir James Hardy.

Sir James recalled to me recently a Brisbane-Gladstone race in which Clem was sailing with a crew of mostly young dinghy sailors. Sensing that he would get neither help with, nor appreciation for, his cooking, he made plans before the start.

He saved some empty Pal tins, the contents of which had been consumed by his dog and smuggled them aboard in his sea bag. The first night at sea, as the fleet ripped out of Moreton Bay and began to heave to the ocean swell, Clem went below to prepare the evening meal – a stew.

Clem Masters on Police Car

Before taking orders from the youngsters on deck, Clem emerged and conspicuously tossed the empty Pal tins overboard.

Clem had very little cooking to do that evening.

Also on the subject of food: Richard ("Sighty") Hammond has vivid memories of the Fastnet race of 1977 – one of the slowest on record – which took Keith Farfor's Australian Admiral's Cup team yacht Superstar seven days to complete.

Before the race, Superstar's crew swallowed the pitch of a swept-up catering service in Cowes run by a pair of attractive "dolly birds" to provision the yacht.

The girls' groceries were more suited to a party than a long sea voyage. A birthday cake and two large bottles of champagne absorbed a large quarter of the 40 pounds per head levy for the food. They also packed a number of quiches, which had to be thrown out after three days.

The crew ended up living on a steady diet: Dry biscuits and lettuce in the evenings, oranges in the mornings.

Only in America

An Australian crew in Long Beach, California, for the annual Congressional Cup match-racing series in 1993, sat down to breakfast on their first day there.

After the waitress ripped through the menu and the bewildering list of options at the usual "diner" breathless pace, the youngest Australian in his best accent asked: "Could you please translate?"

Waitress: "Train's late? The train hasn't run here for years."

Stan's store

EACH YEAR AFTER the Hobart race yachts from the northern ports cruise home with a mix of experienced crew and unknown adventurers. The new mix is always an unknown quantity with the old hands fearing the newcomers might turn out to be chronic sea-sickness sufferers, useless sailors, or have some anti-social habits that will make the long haul unbearable.

Sometimes, however, the system turns up a winner. David Lawson, the experienced navigator who brought Freight Train back to Sydney, told me about Stan, the mystery man, who at first sight looked like a commando with his build and shaven head who did not volunteer too much about himself except that he was a graduate of Terry Wise's Pacific Sailing School in Sydney.

Lawso early on the trip was trying to put a spaghetti Bolognese together but was lacking some ingredients for the sauce. Stan was able to produce them all from his commodious sea bag.

Then, farther up the track, Freight Train's engine became un-cooperative. Again, Stan came to the rescue, this time producing a set of appropriate tools from the bag and the information that he was a qualified diesel mechanic.

By now, he had earned the full respect of the "bilge rats" in the crew who affixed a sign to his bunk: "Stan's fully-stocked store".

Chas's introduction

CHARLES BLUNDELL FROM Tasmania ("Chas from Tas") was highly excited on meeting his old friend from Sydney, Don Mickleborough, who turned up at Malaysia's Raja Muda Cup regatta where Chas was driving the Farr 36 Tara after delivering her from the Philippines.

The regatta, conducted by the Royal Selangor Yacht Club, is an island-hopping series under the hands-on patronage of the Raja Muda (ruler) of Selangor.

Don entered the yacht club with only the lure of a cold beer on his mind, when he was greeted near the door by Chas, who launched into a long and powerful dissertation to a smiling Malaysian accompanying him about what a great and famous ocean racing yachtsman Don was.

When Chas stopped, after about three minutes, to draw breath, Mickleborough intervened to complete the introduction. "And what's your name? he asked the smiling Malaysian.

"I'm the Raja Muda," was the reply.

Contender comeback

THERE WAS SOME hectic racing on the two fresh days during the Contender class world championship at McCrae, Port Phillip Bay, with capsizes and other bad situations abundant.

Sydney sailor John Teasdale had the misfortune to hit a Dutch competitor who was stalled and going backwards, but on starboard tack while Teasdale was on port. The aggrieved Teasdale yelled: "If you think I am going to do a 720 you're bloody well wrong."

The Dutchman made no reply, but just pointed – at Teasdale's mast, hanging over the bow, as the result of a shroud broken in the collision.

Murdoch's tradesman

I HAVE JUST finished reading the William Shawcross biography of Rupert Murdoch. Although I enjoyed it, I was a little disappointed that there was nothing in it about Rupert's yachting exploits with the 18m ketch Ilina in the early 1960s.

Ilina's most notable performance was in 1964 when she set a record time for the 307n mile Brisbane-Gladstone race.

Don Mickleborough, recalling Ilina's preparation for the race, said the crew had many famous names including Jock Sturrock, Norm Wright, Curly Brydon and the renowned tough trio of Raw Meat, Thunder and Earrings.

It also included the Breakfast Creek hotel publican Greg Cavill, who turned up at the yacht with a utility groaning at the axles under a load of beer.

"Ah," said Thunder (Harry Kerslake) appreciatively. "You can always tell a tradesman by the tools."

Syd Fischer's happy birthday

Syd's birthday present

SYD FISCHER'S RAGAMUFFIN won the opening regatta of the 1993 50ft World Cup circuit at Monaco with 1-2-5 placings for the only races completed in light and variable winds.

As everyone knows, Syd is a realist, with nil belief in miracles. But the second in the second race had, he tells me, a touch of the supernatural about it.

Ragamuffin, sixth around the windward mark, looked to be in a hopeless situation as the course was shortened to finish at the end of the run, only 1.5n miles long.

"The first boat went one way, the rest the other and Ragamuffin sailed down the middle and toddled over the line second," said Syd. "It was just a piece of luck.

"Paul Cayard (steering the Italian boat Capricorno) said to us, 'Someone on that boat must be having a birthday!'

"He didn't know and I didn't tell him. But it WAS my birthday," Fischer said.

Russ Evans' fish sandwiches

THE OFFSHORE COMMUNITY was saddened by the loss in 1993 of one of its number, Russell Evans of Melbourne, who sailed 26 Sydney-Hobart races, many of them with his friend Lou Abrahams, who he introduced to the sport.

Russell Evans taught me a long while ago, when he arranged a berth for me on the Warner family's yawl Winston Churchill for some round Port Phillip Bay races that one of the most valuable people you can have on a big yacht offshore is someone who can melt the inevitable tensions between crewmen, as he could.

He was the guy who could break a standoff or defuse the effect of a tantrum, with a quip, a joke, or a gentle reminder that the racing is to be got on with.

Russ also organised a sail aboard Winston Churchill for his friend Lou Abrahams, until then a motor boat owner, who went on to be one of the most successful offshore yacht owner/skippers in Australia.

After skippering Winston Churchill in the 1963 Sydney-Hobart race, Russ joined Lou for his first Sydney-Hobart in 1965 aboard Odin. He went on to sail four more Sydney-Hobarts on Odin, nine more on Vittoria and two on Challenge, all owned by Abrahams.

During the wake at Royal Brighton Yacht Club, it was recalled that Russ was the master of the running gag as well as the short quip. At one time sandwiches were put out on the bar at Royal Brighton for members and their guests on Friday nights.

Kevin Mooney, a friend of Russ' complained through Russ to the management that there were no fish sandwiches for the Roman Catholics.

The management provided fish sandwiches; Mooney continued to complain that there were none. The situation continued for several weeks until the puzzle was solved:

Russ was discovered in the kitchen devouring ALL the fish sandwiches before the tray was conveyed to the bar.

Walking the card

THE PEOPLE WHO sail with Arthur Bloore say he has a dry sense of humour that prevails in the soggiest situations. When his pocket maxi Hammer of Queensland blew out its brand new (up for the second time) 5200sq ft asymmetrical spinnaker in the Lindeman race – the last in 1993 Hamilton Island Race Week – Arthur simply observed: "Looks like we won't have to set that on the next run."

It ranks with his comment in the 1992 Kodak Sydney-Hobart race after the dismasting of Hammer in Bass Strait as darkness fell: "If I had nav lights, I would switch them on."

Arthur's wife Faye responds to Arthur's disasters in a much more practical way. She buys something for the household or herself every time he buys something for the boat.

She was heard to say at a previous Race Week when a sail blew: "I think I'll take the Bankcard for a walk," and headed off for the resort shops.

Bringing the house down

I HOPE THE following was not inspired by the recent advice of Australian Sailing's fitness writer Michael Blackburn recommending trapezing off the side of the house for practice.

From the legendary ranks of the 14-footer sailors comes the story of a lady identified only as "Chrissie the Ballistic Chick".

She had bought a new boat and was itching to get some at-home practice.

She rigged a trapezing simulator between a hook in the ceiling that used to carry a pot plant and a door knob and began trapezing off the wall.

Before her mother could finish saying, "This is not going to work," the ceiling collapsed on Chrissie's head. The new ceiling and the locksmith cost $350.

New outfit

IT'S A FAMILIAR tale. Husband sailor orders a new spinnaker that the boat cannot do without and instructs the sailmaker to have it delivered to his office so the wife will not find out.

But there's a misunderstanding and the sail is delivered to his home instead. The sailor arrives home. The wife, draped in the spinnaker, welcomes him with: "Darling, how did you know I wanted a new wardrobe?"

Australia II's low-tech souvenir

CREWMEN TURNING UP for the Australia II reunion in Perth were invited to bring along bits of the boat and other memorabilia that may have been souvenired after the 1983 America's Cup win.

Chink Longley's contribution was the port winch control button, replaced by Lewmar with a shinier new one when Steve Ward was re-furbishing the boat for its entry into the Maritime Museum.

For the first time, when he dug it out of a box at the Endeavour Project building in Fremantle, Longley noticed that this vital item from the technology-breakthrough boat with its intensive maintenance program had the pin holding it together secured by a paper clip.

Hoddo turns a profit on Lord Howe

CREWS IN THE 1993 Fujitsu Gosford to Lord Howe Island race found a major improvement awaiting them on the hospitable island. The famed watering hole, the Bowling Club, has had a major renovation and re-opened its new bar two days before the racers arrived. It now had draft beer, at reasonable Sydney prices.

A second storey has been added, providing a function room and the roofing replaced with a bull-nosed look corrugated iron that fits well with the heritage status of this most beautiful destinations.

Melbourne Cup day gave the premises a solid workout. It is one of those days when the 280 locals party along in a way that swamps the antics of the most raucous yachties.

Race leader Brindabella had arrived the previous day and David Hodgson, like many of the crew, bought one-dollar tickets in the Melbourne Cup Calcutta as he walked in for a beer.

At the drawing of the Calcutta sweep that night, two of the five tickets Hoddo had purchased were drawn out of the barrel of 1800 or so tickets. Down to his last $10, he sold one for $40 and then proceeded to bid for the horse he held with the other ticket.

As the bidding stretched to $65, he had to borrow a few bucks from crew-mate Tony Hearder to finally secure the horse for $70.

The following day the horse, Te Akau Nick, ran second. Hoddo and Hearder split the $1290 in winnings. Although the locals were not pleased, the windfall enabled Hoddo to stay on at Lord Howe for another two days and plough some of the money back into the local economy.

David Hodgson steering Brindabella on the Lord Howe Island race

Lifebuoy saver

WITH THE MAINSHEET and headsail trimmer occasionally occupied along with the helmsman aboard Brindabella on the almost one-tack Lord Howe race, the boredom on the rail was broken by the usual exchange of life stories and anecdotes.

Bob Fraser recalled the tale of the young boat professional who drew the attention of the owner to a badly cracked lifebuoy and suggested it be replaced.

"Spend, spend, spend; that's all you young fellows can think of," said the owner. "Can't you fix it?"

So the young boat "Nigel" spent two days patching up the lifebuoy with layers of fibreglass. At the subsequent safety inspection, when the lifebuoy was thrown in the water, it sank like a stone.

Australian justice

THERE'S NOTHING NEW about match-racing skippers disagreeing with umpiring calls but Frenchman Bertrand Pace, sailing in the Australia Cup in Perth, couldn't contain his frustration any longer after a series of calls went against him.

"Is that Australian justice?" he shouted at the wise gentlemen in the umpire boat controlling his match.

They just looked at each other. The two umpires were from Japan and New Zealand. The boat driver was Italian.

Soap dodgers triumph

THE WIN BY Adam Gosling's Yes in the resail of race three at the Tag Heuer Etchells world championship on Port Phillip was the best result for the six British boats in the series.

While the Australian competitors would have you believe that it came from a lucky punt to the right-hand corner for a decent lick of new breeze on a patchy day, there is another explanation.

When our editor cruised alongside and asked his old mate David Howlett, middle man on the boat, how the Poms had won, Howlett said:

"Oh, we just didn't wash for a week."

Laser Masters mantra

MASTERS DIVISIONS IN Lasers, for those over 35 who stay in the singlehanded torture machine for the exercise, the camaraderie, or maybe just the beer, continue to be strong throughout Australia.

At the Harwood Island Big River regatta on the Clarence River in the

1994-95 season, the Grand Masters (over 55) division was taken out by Bruce "Stumpy" Keir, reports a correspondent who adds:

"The camaraderie in the Laser Masters is as legendary as the number of legends in it. Said one somewhat bewildered Grand Master to another: "What makes these young fellas go so fast?"

The other paused, then moved closer, looked him straight in the eye and replied: "They're bloody scared you might catch them!"

Clive Roughley retires

CLIVE ROUGHLEY, WHO for longer than anyone on Sydney Harbour could remember raced and cruised his beloved Bluebird Skipjack, had to retire from sailing after the 1994-95 season because of surgery.

Roughley, then 75, bought Skipjack new, 29 years before. "The late Geoff Baker built it in fibreglass and it has stood up to the worst we could do to it," Roughley said.

"The current mast is the fourth, the boom the third, the long spinnaker pole the fourth and the rudder has been rebuilt twice.

"Perhaps this mayhem was caused by our theory that the kite should be carried off the breeze regardless. Using an Etchells kite in a bit of a blow was somewhat hairy but Skipjack tracks dead true on the plane."

The spirit of the boat was inscribed in a plaque on the port bulkhead, which read: "All for one and one for all". There were more inspiring words on a deck beam: "Old age and treachery will overcome youth and skill".

Closing the legend, Roughley said: "And now it is over, leaving us all with memories of great times and great fun and not the least of learning how to ride the wind."

Priscilla Queen of the Ocean

CONTRARY TO WHAT you may have read about the boat being named after a great aunt, Mal Hart's inspiration for his Class C winner in the 1995 Melbourne-Osaka race came from the hit movie featuring transvestites. He and crew Paul Scholten even had team shirts printed proclaiming the title: "Priscilla, Queen of the Ocean".

They boys held a $100 a plate fund-raising lunch at the Mornington pub before the race at which supporters offered various items for auction. A local solicitor offered a free divorce; an accountant a free tax return (Alf Neate bought that). A doctor offered a free medical check-up (a slow-moving item, apparently), restaurants offered free lunches.

"The whole Mornington community got behind us and we raised 12 grand for the day," Hart said.

An unexpected contribution came from Simon Grosser and Cameron

Russell of SP Systems, a Sydney-based material supplier to Hart's yacht-building business. Unable to attend and unknown to Hart and the Mornington folks they paid the expenses from Melbourne to Mornington of two Priscilla type entertainers who introduced themselves as "Simon" and "Cameron" and insisted they sit at the head table with Mal.

It was good laugh at the time and got better. The luncheon party broke up late enough for those who wished to kick on in the bar, including "Simon" and "Cameron".

"It was Friday night and the place was chockers with about 150 tradesmen in there having a drink," Hart said. "These two trannies walked in and you could have heard a pin drop. Two hours later they were dancing on the tables; just like in Priscilla the movie."

Wrongful arrest

ANOTHER ONE OFF the coaster from under the bed: Darwin Evolution was dismasted off North Head less than an hour into the 1995 Sydney-Mooloolaba race.

That meant 15 or so people were back in Sydney that night when their friends, families and neighbours expected them to be away for a few days on the race and its aftermath in Mooloolaba.

One such crewman was early in the evening enjoying a hot shower at his Hunters Hill abode, after the toil of cleaning up the wreckage and contemplating a night out when he was startled by the stern command:

"Police here, we have you surrounded, open up and come out with your hands in the air (or words to that effect; shorthand on beer coasters is notoriously unreliable)."

Our man has good neighbours. They had reported an intruder on the premises. But draped in a towel, explaining the somewhat far-fetched circumstances to the coppers, took all of our hero's aplomb.

James Morrison blows a fanfare

PAT CORRIGAN WHO is a great jazz enthusiast and patron, in his 26th year of continuously sponsoring 18ft skiffs had trumpeter James Morrison make a guest appearance at the launching of his newest one, AEI Pace Express.

James duly poured the champagne over the boat, gave it a trumpet fanfare, then went for a mind-blowing spinnaker run with Steve Quigley and his crew down Sydney Harbour on a 20-25 knot southerly.

This was not too daunting for him as he revealed his sailing background at the launch. It began when he was eight and tried to sail a raft to New Zealand. He sailed Manly Juniors, Lasers and eventually a Flying Dutchman through his years at Pittwater High School and at BYRA.

James Morrison riding AEI Pace Express

At the age of 15 he and his two-years-older brother John, sailed a Laser overnight from Pittwater to The Entrance for a gig the following day. "We had a performance there with Don Burrows and we sent our instruments and clothes on ahead," he recalled.

"We took a Gregory's road map to follow the contours of the coast but didn't realise there's really no entrance to The Entrance; just a bay. We broke the rudder getting ashore through the surf."

Morrison had a one-word response to the ride on the 18: "Fantastic". Soon afterwards, a cascade of trumpet notes echoed across Double Bay Park.

Quitters and winners

"A WINNER NEVER quits and a quitter never wins." First heard at a Laser regatta pronounced by the veteran of the fleet, Graham Gilbert, to one of the younger set, Neville Wittey, when both had been caught on the wrong side of a massive wind shift, were down in the 70s and the temptation to go home was strong.

The expression sounded a bit American at the time, though that was no surprise as Graham, who does business in the States, sails a US-made boat, wears US-style sailing gear and, I suspect, may even enjoy Kentucky Fried Chicken.

However I have since found out the stirring message did not originate with Graham, or even Vince Lombardi or The Fonz but from a professional contest enterer, William Sumners of Brooklyn, New York, who wrote it for a motto contest in 1937.

During a long career of contest entering he won a lot of cash, four diamond rings, three cars, three sets of encyclopaedias, six television sets, five watches, ten radios, two washing machines, one set of golf clubs, one electric fan, two complete wardrobes and 960 cans of tuna.

Though it's disappointing to find the saying has no heroic origin, it's good advice just the same.

From the school of hard knocks

A FAMOUS SYDNEY sailor passed the following along on the basis that his name was not to be used – a measure of the embarrassment as well as the pain the incident caused him.

He was delivering a friend's small yacht from some place to some place on Sydney Harbour alone and in so much wind that he was sailing under headsail only.

After completing a tack, he was settling down at the helm when a gust more severe than most started to blow his hat off.

Instinctively, he grabbed for it. And brained himself with the winch handle he still had in his hand.

As promised, no names. But if you remember seeing a world champion around at the time of the BIG westerlies, with a lump the size of a golf ball on his head, that was him.

1996-2011

'The Admiral' never coughed up the cash
IAIN MURRAY DURING the presentation of prizes for the 1997 JJ Giltinan international championship, at the Australian 18-footers League Double Bay clubhouse, recalled one of the six occasions he won the fabled "soccer ball" trophy, in Auckland.

The year was 1980 when 18-footer sailing was much less professionally driven and rewarded; in those far-off days, especially in New Zealand.

"I opened the prize money envelope and found a cheque for 14 New Zealand dollars. It certainly wasn't wasted," Murray said. "My forward hand Don Buckley promptly ate it."

Joe English's buck's party
JOE ENGLISH, THE noted Irish sailor, pal of Harold Cudmore and humorist, was in town recently, immediately re-kindling some fond memories. He used to sail in a World War Two Nazi helmet, which was useful socially as well. It held a lot of beer, handy for both drinking and throwing.

As the years went by Joe settled down and eventually the time came for his wedding to the lovely and patient April.

There was one last problem as Joe relinquished his freedom. The buck's party was a formal affair in dress terms but became fairly informal as the evening wore on.

Joe, attempting a speech, or jig, or both, fell off a table top and broke his leg. His friends showed little sympathy. When the ambulance men arrived, they found a room full of Irishmen in dinner suits lying on the floor, each clutching a leg and howling.

Eventually they found the real victim but April wasn't too pleased as Joe made it up the aisle on crutches.

Frizzle's can of cheese
THE NOW MARRIED Graham ("Frizzle") Freeman has gone with his lovely wife Kathryn to build catamaran ferries in the Guang Zhou province of China for

Graham Freeman

his Tasmanian school-days friend Robert ("Beanhead") Clifford.

As expected, it sounds like he is having communication difficulties with the locals. Come to think of it, he had communications difficulties when he was living in Australia with his own convoluted usage of rhyming slang, example: "After the Wilson (Picket) we all went Eric (Baume)." Translation: "After the cricket we all went home."

A recent communication to a Sydney friend went: "No Chinas in China to have a silver link with." Translation: No mates (China plates) in China to have a drink with."

Well I do know the man's technique with the chopsticks is excellent and I am sure he will come home eventually fluent in rhyming Can of Cheese (Cantonese).

In the twilight zone
THE SAILING SCHOOL proprietor loaded his students from the tender aboard the J24 for the twilight race. The boat, in the crowded moorings area of the bay, was one he used only occasionally when more students turned up than he could accommodate on the J24s his school owned.

Although he had sailed this boat several times before and knew it to be on the pace with the other Js, this evening its speed was just blinding.

Quickly and effortlessly they burned off the other J24s and made some inroads into bigger boats in the mixed fleet, including some cruiser/racer 30-footers.

Knowing they had the race shot to pieces on handicap, an elated crew and sailing school proprietor returned to the moorings. Only then did he realise that the boat he usually chartered was still sitting on the next mooring in the bay.

'Hello Mum, it's me'
VETERAN OFFSHORE NAVIGATOR John Brooks, a former Commodore of the Cruising Yacht Club of Australia, returned to his Sydney home after spending eight years in Singapore as a pilot for Singapore Airlines.

He got back into sailing through summer, although electing to go harbour racing rather than drag his ageing bones through Sydney Heads once more.

But David Kellett prevailed on him to have another bash out there as navigator of Condor on the Sydney-Mooloolaba race.

He told me on his return home that he enjoyed the race and that little had changed in big-boat sailing offshore except ...

"First night out on deck, I realised something strange and radically different was going on.

"Six of the ten kids stacked on the weather rail were chatting on mobile 'phones; to their girl friends or their mums, I suppose."

Best excuses

THE EDITOR TELLS me that in all his years with the magazine he has had some great excuses for non-delivery of copy and pictures down to the dog eating the manuscript when it was about to be posted.

But he rates the greatest genuine excuse that of Cairns correspondent and fantatical multihull sailor Don Boldiston, who had offered coverage on the Coral Sea Classic.

Don, who was to sail home from Port Moresby on the line honours winning multi Gotcha Covered, explained:

"On the day before I went to Moresby, the hard drive collapsed on my laptop, leaving me with no machine. In New Guinea I was able to access one and get material ready for you on the Coral Sea Classic.

"On the third day out we were boarded by Rascals (pirates). They took my camera with film taken in Moresby plus the article and all my official results and details.

"They even took my guidelines for articles from you. They took everything from my clothes to my recorder. I guess I was lucky not to have my laptop with me as I would have lost it also."

When John Denver's number was up

AMONG THE MANY people around the world devastated by the untimely death of John Denver in 1997 was Terry Wise, proprietor of Pacific Sailing School at the Cruising Yacht Club of Australia, in Rushcutters Bay, Sydney.

Terry had known the American ballad singer for eight years; since the time that Denver during an Australian tour rang the school one day and said he wanted to learn to sail.

"I spent three months sailing with him," said Wise. "We went fishing, too. Fly fishing was one of his great interests. After that, whenever he came out here, he would just take one of our J24s for a sail. When I went to America, I would stay with him and we would go fly fishing."

In 1989, Wise encouraged Denver to join the CYCA as an overseas member. Denver maintained that membership. When he died, habitués of the upstairs bar recalled the night his name was announced as the winner of the lucky badge draw.

"You'll have to yell that out a bit louder," said one. "He's in Aspen, Colorado."

Down and out in deepest St Kilda

THE EDITOR, STAYING in St Kilda during the Sail Melbourne '98 regatta, one Sunday morning was standing in a small queue outside the National Bank's Ackland Street ATM machine. He was behind a large gent who was in a nice suit but wearing no socks and chewing, in absent-minded fashion, on a sandwich.

The suited one completed his transaction and shuffled off.

Just as the editor stepped up to the button end of the business, a lady with a kind face handed him a small card. It read: "Your invitation to a free vegetarian feast, every Sunday 4.30pm, Hare Krishna Temple, 197 Danks St, Albert Park."

The editor tells me the incident shook his perception of what he thought was a suave image in sailing gear: Kenwood Cup tee shirt, neatly pressed denim shorts and Sebago sailing shoes, albeit with no socks.

I told him the Hare Krishna lady's judgment was the right one: A sailing bum looks like any other bum.

Not all dry in Dubai

I'VE JUST LEARNED of a great place to go if you want to get off the grog and drive around a lot. The editor on his return from the ISAF world championships told us all about Dubai. Bored us endlessly, actually, going on about what a great place it was for sailing, safe for tourists, full of warm and wonderful people.

I was a bit interested to know how he got on with his well-known love of beer in this Muslim land. He assured me that the frothy brown stuff was available in hotels, at the Dubai International Marine Club venue for the regatta and at clubs like the Jebel Ali Sailing Club, favoured by expats, just a sand dune away next door.

Drinking in Dubai, however, is quite expensive, unlike the fluid you pour into your car to make it go. After a couple of jars at the Jebel Ali one night, the Falstaffian British yachting writer Bob Fisher offered to drive the editor home.

On the way, Fisher fortunately noticed that they were almost out of petrol. They found a service station off one of the fantastic roads that spear around the desert from Dubai.

The attendant asked whether the preference was premium or standard.

"Hang the expense, premium!" replied Fisher who was in an expansive mood.

Filling the tank cost him 32 dirhams of the local currency – $12.30 in our money, or as the editor pointed out, more than the three beers he had just bought at the Jebel Ali where a schooner costs the equivalent of $4.60.

The Pope, the plumber and the kings

THE GOOD THING about Paul Henderson, the president of the International Sailing Federation, is that he has knocked about a number of different sailing venues as a good competitor in his time and still travels the world-wide constituency in a big way.

Another good thing about Paul Henderson, known universally as "The Pope", is his sense of humour. Addressing the opening session of the Australian Yachting Federation's annual conference in Sydney, he recalled his first meeting as a member of the class policy and organisation council of ISAF.

"All day long, I kept saying to King Constantine, 'your highness, your highness.'

"Somebody came to me and said, 'You had better stop that; he's your majesty.'

Henderson got to know King Constantine very well. He recalled the black tie dinners that were a Thursday night tradition during the ISAF's annual conference in London.

"One year, it was the 80th birthday of King Olaf of Norway, so we made him a big presentation; gave him a model of his 5.5 metre."

Henderson, who has a construction business in Toronto, went on: "The next year, same night happened to be my birthday. I'm a plumber so King Constantine gets up and after talking politely about his plumber friend in Toronto, presents me with a hat with a faucet dripping water.

"So now I have to get up and respond, so I start off with 'My great friend King Olaf of Norway and my great friend King Constantine and my great friend Prince Philip and Crown Prince Harald.

"With that Constantine yells out: 'Name dropper!'"

"Without thinking I said: 'Wadda mean name dropper. I know five kings. You only know one plumber.'"

Should I go?

IT'S A FAMILIAR situation around Hobart race time; the loyal crewman who actually enjoys the race and obviously does not want to let his skipper down is also torn by guilt at having to leave the wife he also loves very much straight after Christmas.

This was the situation facing Nicholas Crawley, a long-time crewman with Grant Wharington on his various Wild Things and at the last possible moment it looked as though the being-with-the-wife option would win over being-with-the-boys on the Wild Thing rail, circa 1992.

Nick decided to stay home and formed a plan to placate the owner. He told his wife Julia early on Boxing Day morning that a sail or some charts for the boat had been left behind and he had to put them on the plane for Sydney.

He drove from Mornington to Tullamarine, selected a position within the terminal that could clearly convey the airport noise and called Wharington to say that he had just missed the plane and could not get on another - "Very sorry, mate."

Wharington, with an extra-sensory appreciation of the situation, immediately called the airline's reservations, found planes for Sydney were leaving every 30 minutes and there were vacancies.

He immediately called Crawley back: "I've booked you on every flight for the next four hours. Get yourself up here!"

So Nicholas Crawley proceeded to Sydney, grabbed a cab to Rushcutters Bay and a ride out on a tender to board the boat between the five- and ten-minute gun, without any sailing gear at all.

Julie Crawley in Mornington, wondering when Nick would return from the airport, idly turned on the television broadcast of the Hobart race start to see her husband sitting on the rail of Wild Thing in his street clothes.

Murphy's Law

ANDREW PALFREY, CREWMAN along with James Mayo for Cameron Miles on an Olympic sailing campaign through Europe in 1999, reported this incident when Miles' Tower Life team was training with Hans Wallen's Swedish crew in Gotskar, Sweden:

"We were sailing downwind in a moderate breeze with the Swedes overtaking on our windward side. Cameron then began to luff the Swedes, who were a little slow to respond. We continued to slow luff and the boats eventually touched, with their bow kissing our port side near the stern.

"As Murphy's Law would dictate their spinnaker pole clipped itself onto our backstay. This could have had a catastrophic effect on the longevity of our mast, but Cameron let go of the helm and rushed to the back of our boat to unclip the pole.

"This took a few seconds and when he eventually freed the backstay it became very slack. As a result, Cameron fell into the water.

"As this was happening, James and I were retrieving our own spinnaker from the sea when we looked up and saw we were about three feet off ramming a Swedish couple in a dinghy who were having a peaceful afternoon fishing.

"James ran up to the bow to fend off. We thought they might be a little terse with us but they had been watching the episode unravel and were hysterical with laughter. There was this three-way tangle of boats, sails, rigging and fishing lines.

"Swedish coach Bjorn eventually picked up Cameron but only after he had captured all of the happenings on his digital video camera (and finished laughing)."

Bonding session

THE BOAT WAS hammering along in the race north, on the edge of controland occasionally wiping out in hard running conditions. The owner's son, who used to sail with his father from Sydney before moving to the Gold Coast, was wishing he was elsewhere and offered to his watch mate: "I'm only out here for some male bonding with my father."

Watch mate: "Have you ever thought of taking him to lunch?"

Carrot-juice set

I LIKED THE description Dan Van Blarcom of the Whitsunday Sailing Club offered an ABC interviewer who asked how the club was coping with the beverage requirements of the 73 competitors in the Asia-Pacific Laser championship as well as the regular crowd of keelboat sailors in Hog's Breath Race Week. The club ran the events concurrently with a minimum of fuss.

"Well," said Dan, "The Laser sailors are the carrot-juice set. They don't hang around much after the racing is over. The Hog's Breath sailors are the rum and beer set. We see heaps of them."

Ross ancestry

GEOFFREY ROSS, OWNER/SKIPPER of 1999 Telstra Hobart race winner Yendys, is incredibly proud of his Scottish heritage; so much so that he went to incredible pains to secure 1836 as the sail number for his new boat.

He explains that 1836 was the year his maternal ancestor Isabella Urquhart arrived in Hobart, on a "free seven-year holiday from a Scottish court.

"She married Frederick Ross, who got there about seven years later under a similar arrangement," said Ross. "He broke a window in London. They both stayed on when they completed their sentences.

"So I just had to have that sail number."

The name game

WHAT'S IN A name? As someone once said and hundreds of someones have been saying since for various reasons. Well there's plenty to be found in boat names if you look around and look hard enough.

61	NZL 546	04	Hells Kitchen
62	AUS 423	72	Men's Shirts, Short Skirts
63	AUS 113	03	Licorice Allsorts
64	USA 575	05	Japingka
65	AUS 319	21	Oil Beef Hooked
66	AUS 235	11	Functional Overlay
67	USA 934	35	Roulette
68	USA 51	02	Smoke & Mirrors

Mysterious boat names

The editor came back with the above photograph he idly snapped in Pittwater on his way to the last race of the 1999 Etchells world championship. And blow me down, in a similar vein; I uncovered the following boat name (left) among the last few strugglers on the result sheet he bought back. You might need to be Irish, or think in Irish, to get the full effect.

The editor also brought back a picture of Peter Alexander perfecting his swing by bashing a few practice balls off the back of his Etchells on the way out to the start – to relieve the boredom of the long tow out to the Palm Beach circle.

I hope Peter's golf card looks better than his Etchells worlds score. He finished ten places ahead of the aforesaid boat with the Irish name, with 233 points.

Discovery in Devonport

The Devonport plaque

DURING THE 2000 America's Cup in Auckland the editor was staying in Devonport at the Esplanade, an old-time hotel that had just been renovated, located handily opposite the ferry wharf.

When he revealed his abode to Auckland acquaintances, one of them volunteered that the Esplanade used to be the favourite watering hole of a famous New Zealand around-the-world Whitbread sailor, who also became renowned locally for another reason.

One day a few years before, a concreting team turned up in the small park opposite the Esplanade to spend some time excavating a deep hole and pouring a slab.

A plaque was secured to the slab, which no-one noticed for a day or two. It's been there ever since. The council will not disturb it for fear of endangering the large tree alongside it.

It is understood that the former Whitbread racer has something to do with the building industry. The editor thought that was just another fanciful waterfront tale until he fell over the plaque one day and took the picture.

Double Dutch

AN E-MAIL FROM "skiffies in Holland" crossed the editor's desk the other day. It had him completely puzzled. Perceiving that I come from a slightly more hip generation he passed it to me and growled: "What do you make of this?"

It read and spelt: "The Dutch hardcore skiffies (one boat is sailing on the Ijsselmeer ...) have read your article on the JJ Giltinan with great pleasure! Your magazine is the only way to get updated on the Aussie skiff scene so is anxiously read.

"However, every year you surprise us when mentioning John Harris's forward hand as Chris Cleary. We all know he is crewed by Craig and Russo! Russo is known here as probably the best forward hand on the scene. We wonder how many Australian skiffies know his real name anyway.

"So please don't confuse Dutch skiffies next time. Call him Russo. Kind regards, Jan Groot."

Well, I told the editor, there is a simple explanation really, not helped by the Dutch misunderstanding of Australia's famous rhyming slang.

Chris Cleary's nickname is in fact "Rissole". And sure, everyone in the 18ft skiff scene knows him by that and appreciates his talents as a funny man as well as a great forward hand.

Glad to have been of assistance.

Edwards tradition

SKIFF TRADITIONS, LIKE the nicknames, never die. The 18-footer replicas Tangalooma and Scot through the past season have been plugging around Sydney Harbour with the Sydney Flying Squadron fleet.

Scot capsized and swamped in a big nor'easter one Saturday and as many 18s did 50-

18ft skiff replica crew await rescue

plus years ago, washed up on Lady Martin Beach, Point Piper, home of the Royal Prince Edward Yacht Club where tradition is also strong and memories long.

John Stuart-Duff, one of the club's older members who still races his Hood 23, saw the plight of Scot's crew. And as members of the Edwards used to do 50-plus years ago, he sent a steward down to the beach with a tray of eight rums for the soggy, swamped Scot sailors.

Measuring in

PETER RENDLE, WHO spent some time on the trailable yacht circuit through the past season, met along the way a couple from Perth who trailed their Court 650 across the Nullabor and through three states to contest various events.

They called him to say while completing the journey from the Marlay Point race, the traffic cops pulled them over on the streets of their home city.

The police queried the width of the boat. At 8ft plus maximum beam it did exceed the limit. One of them put a tape measure across the transom and said: "Only six feet. These things are deceptive, aren't they?"

Would you sail with this guy?

THE EDITOR IN the course of covering the 2000 Australian Etchells winter championship at Mooloolaba ran into Bob Hagan and Bob Fairhall, who sailed together for many years in J24s.

Fairhall, from Newport, was visiting former Newport resident and Royal Prince Alfred YC clubmate Hagan, who now lives on the Sunshine Coast. They are still mates and still do the major J24 regattas together on a boat in which they share ownership.

You would wonder why after the editor, over a couple of beers at Mooloolaba YC, listened to the revelations about sinkings and the great road-show disaster these two buddies have shared, like the time they were towing a boat to a NSW championship at Lake Macquarie YC, the day before the regatta, short of time and automotive power with the towing vehicle a four-cylinder Volvo.

Hagan at the wheel took the opportunity of increasing speed on the dip down to the Moonie Moonie bridge on the tollway. The gravitational force as the rig left the dip and began the ascent was apparently too much for the boat, which slipped back on the trailer.

So, when they levelled out for the more gentle descent to the Ourimbah interchange, the back wheels of the Volvo lifted about a metre clear of the roadway and the whole outfit began to sway uncontrollably.

"I think I've lost it. I'll try to accelerate out of it," offered Hagan.

"Don't touch the brakes," hollered Fairhall, who was silently praying that the tow bar would break free of the tow ball.

The boat resolved the problem by breaking free of its tie-downs, jumping off the trailer and sliding neatly on its side past the car to come to rest quite conveniently outside an emergency 'phone.

The damage didn't look too bad, apart from the 3cm ground off the keel and the 45 degree bevel put on the masthead. Hagan's first reaction, according to Fairhall, was, "Where can we get another boat?"

They were a bit nervous about the first car that pulled up on the scene because it was occupied by a crown sergeant of police on his way home. But instead of raising questions about the weight of the towing vehicle in relation to the trailer-borne load, he said: "Is this one of those J24s. I've got a Bluebird. I'd like to have a sail on a J24. Well you seem to be under control," and drove off.

Almost miraculously a tow-truck driver within half an hour organised a crane that restored boat to trailer. As the crane lifted the boat, the realisation came that the keel had ended up at an angle of 20 degrees.

It swung back neatly to vertical as the crane lifted the boat onto the trailer.

At the lake, a lot of bog temporarily fixed it in place and the Hagan/Fairhall team placed second in the championship.

Wait, there's more. The week before that, Hagan, Fairhall and crew had sunk the same boat off Barrenjoey in a club race. A "microburst" wind gust capsized and pressed the upturned boat down for a minute and a-half.

Fairhall, with a soggy ten dollar bill in his pocket available for a cab fare home, began swimming for shore. "Wait," said Hagan. "No-one's leaving this sinking ship." So the five crew members clung to the bow, kept just above water by an airlock, until a salvage operator turned up to tow them in.

The boat sank as the tow began but was raised undamaged that afternoon with its winches full of sand and a ruined Sailcomp compass, but otherwise okay.

Hagan and Fairhall shared another shipwreck while training for the 1994 J24 nationals on Botany Bay. With young Julian Plante on the bow, they were practising spinnaker gybes when a gust totally inverted them and stuck the masthead in the bottom.

A police boat

Bob Hagan (left) and Bob Fairhall, still mates

towed them onto a mud flat just outside the Captain Cook Bridge. They pumped and bailed as much water out of the boat as they could and waited for the tide to refloat it. But as the tide rose, they realised the boat was plugged into the mud by the keel and was swamping again.

A boatshed operator arrived with his diving gear, swam into the boat with a pump and filled the bow area with air. The boat re-floated on the tide and the Hagan/Fairhall crew went on to win the national championship.

A spell in the Etchells class also fell short of being disaster free for Hagan and Fairhall. During the 1993 world championship in Brisbane they were trying on port to weave through the starboard tackers approaching a windward mark.

Next thing, Fairhall was aware of the bow of another boat riding up on the gunwale and over his head. But he did not realise that it had also hit the mast two metres above the deck and snapped it in two.

"Quick, do a 720," said Fairhall after the boats slid apart.

"Have a look up," said Hagan.

The house that George built

GEORGE MOTTL DECIDED in 2000 to sell his quite unusual house on Scotland Island on Scotland Island in Pittwater, Sydney. George in 1988 seriously rebuilt the house from an earlier small cottage and boatshed on the site.

He was a yacht broker, operating from Church Point right opposite at the time and also a boatbuilder, remembered mostly for his Mottle 33 aft-cabin cruising boats.

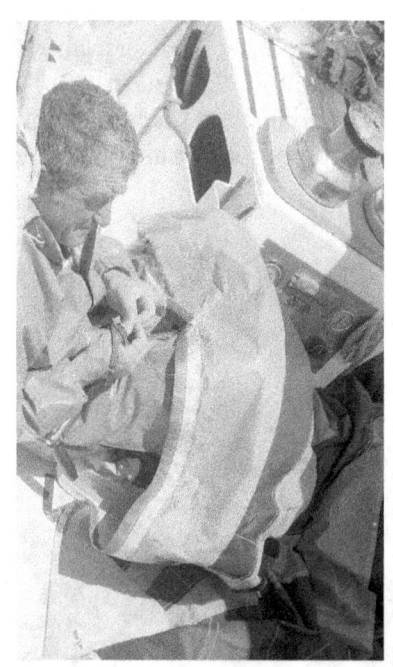

George Mottl

George was also a keen and very good offshore racing sailor with the experience and respect for the forces of nature making him a sought-after crewman and skipper.

Not surprisingly, the house George built reflected his love of sailing boats. He crafted 80 square metres of living space from Australian hardwood timbers and incorporated some nautical ideas.

The downstairs area is largely open plan, overlooking the private jetty and with the panoramic view of Pittwater. In a corner, the kitchen is a wooden replica of a typical but big L-shaped yacht galley. It's a kitchen built for entertaining where the chef (George, when he is residence) participates in the conversation flow.

The bathroom is very similar to a yacht's

head and serves also as a laundry. The two bedrooms upstairs, which have more panoramic views and the loft, for unexpected guests and children, are reached by companionway-style ladders; tricky after the good wines at dinner.

George's commuting adventures, between Scotland Island and Church Point, are as legendary around Pittwater as the house itself.

One night, while ferrying some finely-clad dinner guests back to the mainland, he drove his outboard "tinny" clean under and joined them in the swim to shore.

Another evening a Scotland Islander, walking down the Church Point jetty to the aluminium dinghies many of them used to make the last stage of the homeward journey, in the darkness noticed a pair of white-knuckled hands clinging to the jetty's edge.

It was George. In trying to climb from the jetty into the dinghy underneath, he'd accidentally kicked it loose and remained stuck, hanging there.

"My dinghy is drunk," he explained to the rescuer.

Andy goes cruising

DURING THE WHITSUNDAY regattas in 2000 I bumped into Andrew Moncrief, retired from his hands-on management of his Sydney boatbuilding business to go cruising.

He had delivered a boat north and was sailing on her in Hamilton Island Race Week. Andy explained his new cruising lifestyle philosophically: "I've gone from being knee deep in shavings to knee deep in bottle tops."

Flinders Island wisdom

I WAS SO miffed at my column getting chucked out of the January 2000 issue to make way for a long letter about the boat show that I retreated to one of my favourite places in Australia, Flinders Island (not to dry out as the editor of this magazine has been telling everyone).

But one day, I have to admit, I was badly stuck with something to do before the tavern opened at Lady Barron.

Wandering around, I came upon the general store; the only store, really, so it had everything. In the store I found a bookcase of pre-loved books "sold on behalf of the Anglican Church funds, donations gratefully accepted."

On that shelf I found a book for which I paid the 50 cent marked price – Darcy Niland's Australian classic Dead Men Running.

Also on the shelf was Writing for Profit in Australia, obviously passed on as useless by the previous owner and alongside it, Relief for Arthritis. I cheerfully donated another 15 cents to the church and left both books on the shelf, knowing from bitter personal experience that there is no such thing as writing for profit in Australia, or relief from arthritis.

'Big Bad's' boats

LET ME DECLARE before going any further my policy of accepting in the course of my duties only those gratuities, gifts, bribes that cannot be eaten or drunk within 24 hours.

So firstly, here's how a windfall of eight schooners came my way recently down at the members' bar of the Cruising Yacht Club of Australia.

One evening there, not in my presence, well-known leeward runner trimmer Tony Cable, who is also one of the club's historians, declared extravagantly that the late John Gilliam, known everywhere as "Big Bad", had owned 50 boats.

"No way, said Bob ("Sir Robbo of Queensland") Robertson. It would be more like 12. I am so certain about this that I will buy you a schooner for every boat he owned over 12 if you will buy me five schooners for every boat under 12."

So Cable spent a good portion of the following week going through 90 old issues of the club's Offshore magazine. Around the 87th, from 1974, he came across an article about Big Bad's 27th boat and so knew he was on the right track.

But his trail ended there and so he began frantically ringing around other journalistic sources, including me. And would you believe, Australian Sailing in its July 1981 issue had an article by the editor headlined: "Big Bad's 30th boat", that enabled me to cut a deal with Cable on getting a piece of the action with Sir Robbo.

It related how in 50 years of sailing Gilliam, who was then 70, had owned 30 yachts. "Some of them were Sydney-Hobart winners; some he has owned twice; some he has difficulty remembering at all. He cannot bear to be without a boat," the article said.

John began his sailing in Melbourne, like many others in an 18ft Jubilee, the Charlie Peel one design that had a strong following in Sydney as well as Melbourne. She was called Revellie and he thought he paid 105 pounds for it.

Among the yachts he owned twice was Tarni, a 57ft Alden design known as

John Gilliam with a model of Tarni.

Kurrewa III when the Livingston brothers, Frank and John, owned her. Another was Wild Wave, designed by Jock Muir and built in Hobart for bothers L. and G.Keats. She finished first in her first Hobart race only to be disqualified for a starting line collision.

Yachts he owned after moving to Sydney included Siandra, which won the Sydney Hobart race twice, in 1958 and 1960 for her original owner Graham Newland.

He sailed four Hobart races on Weatherly, his steel version of the Halvorsen brothers' famous Freya design. Then he bought Koomooloo, the Hobart race winner in 1968; then Mercedes III, Ted Kaufman's Admiral's Cup triallist and then Aggression, a 43-footer.

His 30th boat, Restless, was a Cavalier 975 stock production 32-footer. I believe Restless was Big Bad's last boat but I'm not certain. Anyone who knows of more can pick up a lazy schooner any time from Cable and Sir Robbo. I've already had my share.

Chris Nicholson's off pasta

AFTER SAILING ALMOST halfway around the world in the 2001-2002 Volvo race, Australian 49er skiff Olympian Chris Nicholson was still not certain that he wanted to be an ocean racer.

He was still struggling with seasickness at the start of each leg, a condition not assisted by being the boat's electrician and having to get his head stuck in wiring and junction boxes below decks at times while Amer Sports One was bucketing along.

"It's almost controllable," he said on arrival in Sydney. "I am sick for two or three days in the leg and then just get better and better. I am able to continue working (trimming and steering) despite that; otherwise I would not go on."

Physically the first two legs – the longest in the race at 7350n miles from Southampton to Cape Town and 6100 from Cape Town to Sydney through the freezing, iceberg-studded Southern Ocean – have taken toll on bodies and probably minds as well. The sailors who arrived in Sydney looked fresh and fit as they stepped off their boats; still running high on adrenalin. Two days later, some of them were shuffling around their maintenance chores like zombies.

Nicholson, who is slim anyway, said he had lost 6kg on leg two and admitted to feeling washed out. Before the start of the race in Southampton, he was fit enough to do 30 chin-ups on the overhead bars in the gym. "In Cape Town I could only do eight chin-ups. Now, I reckon I could do three."

Nicholson arrived in Sydney with no feeling in his toes, a legacy of leaking sea boots that had left his feet in a residue of water at temperatures down to three degrees. The doctor at a compulsory medical inspection for the crew told him he had "trench foot"; the condition our grandfathers endured in the trenches of World War One.

While everyone one board had been conscious of the need in the interests of nutrition to take on 6000 calories a day, Nicholson's interest in eating was set back when he discovered one of the duty cooks straining the pasta in the toilet bowl – the only possible option in some extreme conditions.

The bride got the blame

Michael Coxon, the very promising young 18ft skiff sailor, faced a problem. A heat of the 2002 JJ Giltinan international series on Sydney Harbour overlapped with the wedding of his brother Alex in North Sydney.

So as he finished the race young John Winning, the new 29er world champion, jumped on Coxon's boat, Daily Telegraph, to steer it ashore. Coxon boarded the Palm Beach "gentleman's" launch owned and steered by John Harris.

Coxon cleaned up under the transom shower on the cruiser and changed into his wedding finery as Hanger Harris sped to Lavender Bay. Coxon walked as briskly up to the church but still arrived three minutes late.

But he was excused, at least by his mother Bev, who just said, "How inconsiderate of the bride to arrive on time."

Darcy Harvey chugs on

When Port Lincoln Yacht Club identity Darcy Harvey celebrated his 80th birthday party in 2002, the club's Holdfast trainer class group gave him a surprise party. And why wouldn't they? Darcy had been their starter and mentor for 42 years. He had conducted at least 615 races from his faithful motor boat Chugga.

Harvey, born in bred in Port Lincoln, had been a member of the club since 1933 and was awarded life membership in 1956.

He gave up competitive sailing in 1960 when his eldest son Neil, who was ten, began sailing in the junior Holdfast trainer class at the club.

Neil and his younger brother, Michael, who also went through the program went on to become America's Cup and maxi boat sailors. Both live in the USA where Neil is southeast manager for Harken, based in Florida and Mick, a long time member of Dennis Conner's America's Cup shore teams, settled in Newport, Rhode Island.

Darcy won Chugga, a half-cabin Hartley launch, in a Christmas raffle at the club with a five quid ticket in 1961. The original marinised Ford 10 motor ("crank and go, no gears") was replaced in 1972 by a Yanmar MTS85 salvaged from a sunken fishing boat, which emits the sound that led to the boat's name.

While the editor and I were in Port Lincoln for the finish of the Adelaide-Lincoln race and the start of the Lincoln Week regatta in 2002, we caught up with Darcy who was variously cooking breakfast for the sailors, wading through a mound of garbage from the Adelaide-Lincoln presentation lunch and barbecuing again after the Lincoln Week races. The garbage sorting was part of his regular recycling of cans and bottles to generate finances for the Holdfast program.

A regular feature on Lincoln's sailing social calendar is the Thursday night shed party at the home of Darcy and Verlie Harvey. The trusty back shed is set up with a bar and decorated with flags, posters, photographs and other memorabilia sent home by Mick and Neil Harvey.

A regular there is the giant boat deliverer Megga Bascombe. While I was in Port Lincoln, Megga 'phoned Darcy from an airliner 39,000ft over the Java Sea to let him know that he had, with the help of the pilot, located an island where Darcy served with M Force behind enemy lines in World War Two. Megga was on his way to Malaysia to deliver Helsal II back to Australia.

Darcy Harvey barbecuing at Lincoln Week

Because of secrecy provisions, few people, not even family members, have learned much about Darcy's service as an acting corporal, scout and guard with M Special Unit Allied Intelligence Bureau.

His party of six was landed on Sakala Island, behind Japanese lines, by an American submarine and spent eight months there tracing Japanese troop, air and naval movements and identified where the POW camps were, although two of their Malay forward scouts were caught by the Japanese and beheaded.

Malay fishermen eventually betrayed the group to the Japanese who sent planes and a gunboat to try and find them. In response to their radio appeal for rescue, a Catalina flying boat arrived. With two Liberator bombers as escorts, the Catalina had to taxi seven miles before it could get airborne and head for Darwin.

It flew just above the waves most of the way to avoid enemy fighters and was attacked by night fighters over southern Java.

In 2010, Darcy received the Order of Australia Medal for his services to junior sailing, Australian Rules football and the community. Neil Harvey, who attended the award ceremony with Darcy at Government House, Adelaide, recalled that while Darcy was behind enemy lines he survived on "monkey tails, bamboo shoots and rice. The latter was and to this day is still forbidden at our house in Port Lincoln."

Best bilge cleaner

DURING A TWILIGHT race on Sydney Harbour, the part owner of a Hood 23 somehow lost a treasured adornment – a diamond stud that he usually sports in an ear, valued at $10,000.

As a result, that Hood 23 has the cleanest bilge of any boat on Sydney Harbour, although the stud has yet to be found. Possibly it dropped into the cockpit and drifted through a drain, or maybe bounced over the side.

As the bilge search for the diamond stud continued, other Hood 23 owners who heard of its loss have begged me not to reveal the name of the boat. As a consequence of the loss, they reckon, the second-hand value of every Hood on the harbour has risen by $10,000.

Rime of the Ancient Mariner

Water, water, everywhere,
And all the boards did shrink;
Water, water, everywhere,
Nor any drop to drink.
– Samuel Taylor Coleridge

AN ANCIENT MARINER told me about a water shortage that has nothing to do with the current Australian drought. He is an experienced sailor and a good navigator who was charged with delivering a 60-footer to the Whitsundays.

The crew was a mix of the boat's old hands and some newcomers, including some youngsters who had never been to sea before. Before departing Sydney, he gathered everyone (he thought) together and impressed on the youngsters the importance of conserving water.

Mysteriously, despite an extremely fast passage on a fresh southerly front from Sydney, he realised the water supply was running out. A diversion to Southport had to be made to top up the tanks. At sea again, the water supply continued to fall alarmingly.

Then it hit him. The one crew member who had not been at his pre-voyage lecture – stranger to the boat but a mature, responsible-looking type who sailed regularly on the harbour – was spending an inordinately long time over ablutions each morning. Yep, he'd been having the ten-minute hot shower he enjoyed at home.

About that time the discovery was also made that the water taken on in Southport was from the wrong source on the dock and was not of drinkable quantity.

So rationing began, to the displeasure of one of the veterans who just could not get by without his regular fix of coffee. By the time they reached Hamilton Island, he had become impossibly irritable.

But he raised a laugh, with the rest, when they unloaded the bricked racing sails from the boat's second toilet and found, underneath the sails, two cases of bottled water – two-litre bottles at that!

Courtesy lesson

MOST OF THE regulars sailing on Sydney Harbour will be familiar with the scenario. An almost out-of-control 18ft skiff, careering down the harbour screaming obscenities at all craft in her path – without being too certain about what that path is.

A friend of mine, who sails a Laser, recently decided enough was enough. While racing, he called starboard on an 18-footer under spinnaker that was actually on the way to the start of its race on the other side of the harbour.

From the 18 came the reply: "I don't see you!"

My mate, enraged at the arrogance, took revenge. He clamped an iron grip on the dangling leeward tiller extension and would not let go until the 18 cartwheeled into a capsize.

'Cripes that's piss'

FROM DON MICKLEBOROUGH'S archival memory: Two of Rubber Kellaway's mates from the early days of "maxi" ocean racing aboard the Livingston brothers' Kurrewas and the 18ft skiffs, were Joe ("Raw Meat") Pearce and Harry ("Thunder") Kerslake.

One day on Raw Meat's skiff, they were near becalmed, only just stemming the tide, trailing a boat skippered by one "Skinny" Cole, who Raw Meat and Thunder regarded as a mean-spirited person.

They saw Skinny Cole drop a half-full flask-sized rum bottle into the water and as it drifted towards them, Skinny motioned that they should have a drink. "He's not such a bad bloke after all," said Raw Meat, taking a substantial swig.

"Here, save some for me," said Thunder.

Thunder swigged and spluttered, "Cripes, that's piss."

"Yeah I know," said Raw, "I didn't want to be the only one caught out."

Sighty the leopard

I was fortunate enough to be a guest at the party Richard ("Sighty") Hammond and his family staged to celebrate Sighty's 70th birthday in 2003. There were some great stories on the night, which turned out to be somewhat a Sighty roast.

Sighty Hammond, behind Alan Bond at the helm, 1973

On an early Admiral's Cup campaign in England, a young and always playful Sighty Hammond was with the Australian team, staying at The Quarterdeck, a private hotel in Cowes, where a strict curfew applied on the team.

He was seated in the lounge when an unidentified crewman returned late one night with a female companion.

The proprietor of The Quarterdeck fancied himself as a big game hunter and a leopard skin adorned the lounge room wall. Sighty took down the leopard skin, put it on and enlisted a couple of other crew members to be his "growlers".

They sneaked upstairs into the bedroom where the errant crewman and his companion were getting to know each other and gave them such a scare that they bolted into the street.

Sighty and the growlers decided to work the same dodge on another crewman who was asleep upstairs. This guy woke in fright and jumped straight on the "leopard", so heavily that he cracked two of Sighty's ribs, which left him out of action for a couple of days.

A couple of Fleet Street journalists got onto the story. Why wasn't the top Australian navigator on board his boat? Sighty, more than a bit embarrassed by this, did not make it clear to the birthday gathering whether he told a fib, or was on the end of a piece of journalistic licence. But he was much relieved when the papers came out with headline, "Australian navigator injured in fall down hatch."

Bit of a man overboard

Life Without Limits, David Pescud's autobiography by Helen O'Neill, tells of Pescud's struggle to make his way in life with dyslexia, unable to read or write and concludes with the story of Sailors with disAbilities, the program that Pescud and Phil Vardy founded in 1994, to encourage disabled people to go sailing.

Sailors with disAbilities crew from left back: Alby Burgin (coronary impaired), David Pescud (dyslexic), Cathy Josling (trainer), Richard Bowler (Parkinsons disease), Clive Gregory (single leg amputee), Allan Grundy (polio). Front seated: Simon Forbes (double leg amputee), Michael Terren (paraplegic), Harold Mirlieb (deaf), and Albert Lee (double leg amputee).

While preparing Pescud's Carpe Diem for the 1994 Sydney-Hobart race, the disabled crew had some sessions with a Tasmanian film maker. It was a sensitive time for the SWD team, who still had to convince the race-organising Cruising Yacht Club of Tasmania that it was able-bodied enough to contest the 50th Sydney-Hobart race.

Life Without Limits records: "The plan was to do a gybe. There were two cameramen on the boat, shooting our one-leg-below-the-knee amputee John Woodward as he stood on deck and handled the ropes, and another in frog suit in the ocean ahead of the us; ready to film the bow of the boat as it ran towards him and over him.

"The gybe began and all was going smoothly. John was standing on deck as the boom moved across and the boat started to take the wind in her sail.

"Suddenly a rope got coiled around John's prosthetic leg. It took up the weight and whipped the leg off, leaving John shocked but still somehow upright.

"The prosthesis flew up high above the mast, doing circle after slow, lazy circle as we watched in stunned silence. It was just about to hit the water when Al Grundy yelled out: 'Bit of a man overboard!'"

Pescud, believing the CYCA would not let them into the Hobart if he saw the footage, stormed up to the director and told him it must never be released.

"By the time the frogman in the water had crawled out to let us know he had never seen anything so strange, we were all wetting ourselves with laughter. My threats must have done the trick. It never did get used in the documentary; that footage. Or leggage, should I say?"

Engraved winch handles
FORMER ROYAL PRINCE Edward Commodore and racing rules expert Doug Talty tells me that fellow club member Richard Cortis has the winch handles on his boat engraved with crew members' names.

"In gratitude for their services?"

"No," said Doug. "Each records the name of a crew member who has lost a winch handle overboard. It is engraved on the replacement."

As a result, repeat offences are apparently rare.

Charter chatter
A REGULAR AND constant source of amusement for Whitsunday residents is the radio traffic between novice hirers and the bareboat charter company bases.

One couple radioed in reporting that they had run out of anchors. They had used up all three that came with the boat, but were out on a five-day cruise and needed two more.

Another charter radioed in reporting, "We have run out fuel, but don't worry, we have topped up from the tank in the dinghy for the outboard."

"Have you tried to start the motor?"

"No."

"Whatever you do, don't! Someone will be with you shortly."

Any complaints? Call this number ...
HAMILTON ISLAND RACE Week founders David Hutchen, Warwick Hoban and Leon O'Donoghue got together for a reunion during the 20th running of the event in 2003 and so the stories flowed.

The event and the world in general almost lost Hoban, then regatta director in 1995 when he had a serious skiing accident at Falls Creek. During the regatta that year he was laid up in traction, with a severely injured back, in Albury Base Hospital.

Gamely, he volunteered to handle the handicapping duties, with the help of a laptop, from his bed of pain.

Hutchen, believing that Hoban might be feeling left out of things while the regatta was in progress, wrote in his welcoming message to competitors in the regatta program: "Anyone with complaints about their handicap should ring Warwick Hoban on this number ..... (giving Hoban's bedside telephone number at the hospital).

"Everybody rang me," said Hoban. "It became more than a joke. I was in a four-bed room and when the 'phone went the others would say, 'not someone else wingeing about their handicap?'"

The following year Hoban, back on his feet and at the island again in the race director's role, got his own back on Hutchen, again in the regatta program.

Hoban wrote that anyone with complaints about noise at night should ring the following number..... (giving Hutchen's room number for the week at the resort hotel).

Warwick Hoban

Again, the 'phone ran hot as more people got in on the gag. Hutchen was surprised at how much noise was reported at 4am when he couldn't hear a thing.

Good to see that they are still firm friends.

Official: Chas from Tas an Aussie

THE MAYOR OF Whitsunday Shire, Councillor Mario Demartini, in a simple ceremony at Airlie Beach in 2003 declared Charles Phillip Blundell to be an Australian citizen, ending a bureaucratic saga that kept "Chas from Tas" in nationality limbo for many years.

Internationally, Chas has been of Australia's best-known sailors and ocean-racing crewmen. For 25 years, many of them with Chas based in Hong Kong and the Philippines, he delivered and raced yachts all over the world, some famous ones among them including Phantom, Sorcery, Windward Passage, Nirvana, and Charisma from the USA; Yeoman XXI and Yeoman XXIII with British Admiral's Cup teams.

He was a survivor of the roll-over of Simon le Bon's maxi Drum, fortunately within sight of land and reach of rescuers when she lost her keel off the coast of Cornwall in the 1985 Fastnet race.

More recently, Chas was seriously injured in an assault at a nightclub in the Philippines. While Chas is the steadiest of sailors afloat, with a wonderful affinity for the ocean and its moods, he has encountered difficulties in social life ashore.

Flown home to Hobart by his caring family, he recovered in Royal Hobart Hospital, recuperated in Tasmania, studied for sea-going qualifications at the Australian Maritime College in Launceston and went to live in Airlie Beach, from where he began working on a tourist dive platform on the Great Barrier Reef.

Through all of this, despite the name, Chas from Tas was never an Australian citizen. Although he had returned to Australia a dozen times since his departure in 1969 to take up a position with Rothmans in the UK, he had been required to obtain an entry visa on the British passport he carried each time he returned to Australia.

Chas was a British subject, born in Devon, who came to Australia in 1951, aged three, with his family. His father became involved in dairy farming and fishing in Tasmania and Chas grew up on his father's farm at Woodbridge on the shores of the D'Entrecasteaux Channel.

He had a good education, although I only learned from him recently how he had become a boarder at The Friends School in Hobart at the age of ten. His parents sent him there after they found he had "wagged-it" for two and a-half weeks from the local primary school to go fishing and sell the fish on the roadside.

On completing his education at Hobart Matriculation College, Chas went fishing again – commercially – on boats working in Tasmanian and South Australian waters, from 1965 to 1968 before joining Rothmans of Pall Mall in Victoria. At the age of 22, he left Australia in late 1969 to take up a position with Rothmans in the UK.

He became involved in professional sailing, initially working for six months in the Mediterranean as mate aboard the Fyfe 86 Carlina. He then sailed to the Caribbean in the crew of Sir Max Aitken's Crusade to establish a transAtlantic status that kept him on the move between England and America for the next ten years.

While Chas was absent from Australia, all his family became Australian citizens. He believed that although he held a British passport, he was also an Australian citizen. He was unaware of the law change during the Whitlam era that made retaining residence status after an absence of more than three years from Australia, was not allowed.

Settling back in Australia would not be easy without citizenship. Over several years Chas's family and Australian friends headed by Sydney-based Tasmanian Don Mickleborough, campaigned in support of Chas's application for residency and citizenship.

The process was complicated by Chas's nomadic wanderings abroad, worldly possessions in two sea bags, the bureaucratic situation far from his thoughts until the Philippines incident put him "on the beach" and in serious need of the benefits of Australian residency and citizenship.

Chas is extremely proud of his Australian citizenship medal and wishes to thank all who supported his application. During 2003 Hog's Breath Race Week and Hahn Premium Hamilton Island Race Week, Chas was able to thank his supporters, including some of the South-East Asian expats who helped him greatly on the road to recovery.

Among them was Dr Ian Nicholson from Hong Kong, who skippered his Warwick 60 Intrigue of Stornoway to win performance handicap division one in the Hog's Breath regatta at Airlie Beach.

Chas spent a day sailing aboard Intrigue of Stornoway at Hamilton Island, but left the regatta early for that most important engagement with Mayor Demartini.

JJG bomb scare

THE JAMES J. Giltinan Trophy was presented by Giltinan, then secretary of the NSW Sailing League, for a world championship in 18ft skiffs to coincide with Sydney's 150th anniversary in 1938.

It is one of the world's most unusual sporting trophies. A globe of the world has cut-outs, in which repose intricate models of 1930s 18s.

The League placed advertisements inviting entry to the event in major newspapers around the world. It received replies from England, USA, Hong Kong and New Zealand, including expressions of interest from America's Cup identities Harold Vanderbilt and Sir Thomas Sopwith. But due to the war clouds gathering over Europe, only the New Zealanders were able to compete.

An Australian skiff, Bert Swinbourne's Taree, won. The carnival was a great success with the total crowd watching from spectator ferries, boats and foreshore of Sydney Harbour estimated at more than 10,000.

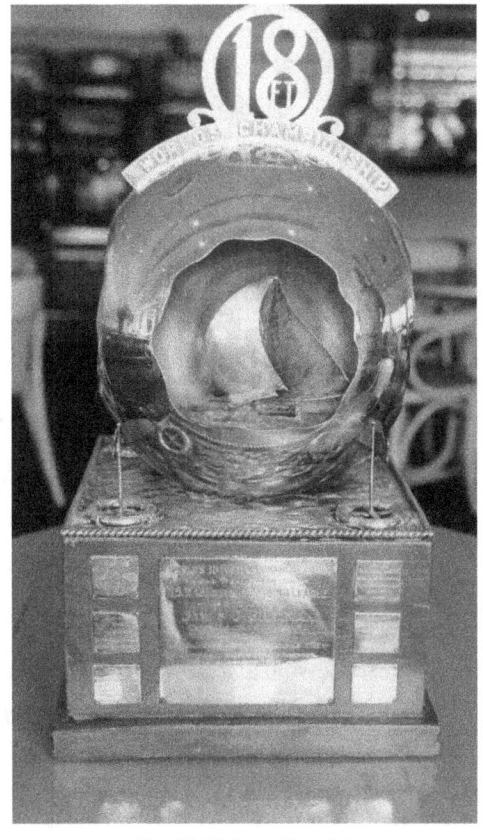

The JJ Giltinan "bomb"

The New Zealand M-class 18-footer Manu won the 1939 contest in Auckland. Competition resumed after the war in 1948 and the JJ Giltinan international championship has remained the 18s premier competition.

Apart from a brief sojourn in New Zealand, the trophy stayed in the League's trophy cabinet, pulled out only for the prize giving at the end of the end of the annual Giltinan series, until 1997.

That year, at the instigation of Australian entrepreneur Adam Wilson, a world championship was staged in Sardinia, with the JJ Giltinan trophy at stake. The League gave board member Keith Piggin the responsibility of taking the trophy, valued at $25,000, to Sardinia and back.

Although the trophy is extremely heavy, Keith elected to take it in a bag as hand luggage, determined that the irreplaceable artifact would be in his possession the whole time on the journey.

All went well until the Australian team flew from Rome to Nice on a smaller 727 commuter aircraft. The Australians had so much hand luggage; airline staff insisted that it all be stacked at the back of the plane.

At Nice airport, the passengers had to take a bus from the plane to the terminal. "I asked the guys to pick up the trophy as well as their hand luggage," Piggin said. "I got on the bus, no trophy.

"I was absolutely freaked out. I jumped off the bus, and then I saw the bag sitting on the tarmac with four security guards surrounding it. They thought it could have been a bomb!"

Not in my shoes

THERE WAS ONE cloud over Australian 18-Footers Sailing League's successful 2003-04 season in which younger crews began to challenge the class veterans Trevor Barnabas and John Winning.

Regular theft began from the gear bags of clothing the crews tended to leave hurriedly pushed under their trailers in Double Bay park after the usual last-minute rush to rig for the breeze on the day.

Then one Sunday, sailors returning ashore after the race, spotted the thief in the act. A bunch of them chased him up the road and collared him as he tried to scale a wall.

One of the sailors, who happened to be a policeman, held the miscreant in the approved fashion throughout a struggle until on-duty police arrived.

Grant Rollerson, who skippered Fisher & Paykel with the League fleet that season, was pleased to note that the alleged offender (police speak for innocent until proven guilty) was wearing the shoes that had gone missing from Rollerson's bag three weeks earlier.

Valhalla bound

GOOD TO HEAR that a plentiful supply of "mutton bird repellent" was downed at the Cruising Yacht Club of Australia by former crew mates of Oddy Karlsen after his funeral recently.

Odd William Karlsen's physical strength was legendary when he sailed on the 1973 Sydney-Hobart line honours winner Helsal, the ferro-cement "Flying Footpath". He was known in the 'seventies as "the human cleat".

Cancer in recent years, which left him without a lung, may have levelled him physically but did not damage his sense of humour or love of his homeland, Norway.

He proudly proclaimed himself to be a senior Viking while identifying his son Kristian as "the junior Viking" and daughter Analisa as "a junior Viking in training".

After all, he had been one of the two young sailors from the corvette KNS Acanthus to hoist the Norwegian flag to mark the German surrender at Marineholm, Bergen, in 1945.

Through his long illness, Oddy continued to race Wednesday afternoons on Sydney Harbour and entertain, afloat and ashore, with tall stories from the time he was a "sardine harpooner", enhanced by the slow drawl of the Norwegian accent.

Oddy may not have invented mutton bird repellent, a mix of rum and bitter lemon – for a time a popular drink at the CYCA's Coasters Retreat bar – but took credit for the name.

"Does it work?" recipients would ask as they sipped the powerful brew.

Oddy would reply: "Well, have you seen any mutton birds around here lately?"

Hosties 1 – Mickleborough 0

A TABLE OF veteran crewmen who had sailed on Don Mickleborough's ancient sloop Southerly at a CYCA prawn and trivia night with the Sydney-Hobart race as the principal theme, lost on a tie-breaker.

Not surprisingly, with Southerly's motto "old age and treachery will always beat youthful exuberance," Mickleborough then suggested to master of ceremonies Peter Shipway that a prize should be awarded to the table whose occupants had the biggest tally of Hobart race participation.

Mickleborough had already calculated that his table had a total of 191 and was confident of success.

Shipway, craftily perhaps, posed the question to the room as: "Which table has been to Hobart most times?"

A table of former air hosties organised by Marion Alexander, right next to Mickleborough's, shot up their hands and walked off with the three bottles of wine. Yes, they had been to Hobart several thousand times

Electrifying

LASER WORLD, THE International Laser class magazine, carried a report from Jack Schlacter of the Gosford Sailing Club of a terrifying lightning strike:

"Chris Meech, a Laser sailor for over 20 years, got the best lift of his sailing career recently and can probably claim a world record for lifts. Chris got lifted clear out of his boat and landed ten metres away when he was struck by lightning.

"We were sailing home after a race had been abandoned due to a thunderstorm heading our way. I was steering with two fingers holding the rubber stopper at the end of my tiller extension, heading for the nearby tall masts of moored yachts when I felt a sharp tingle through the tiller.

"I looked around to see Chris hanging motionless in his life jacket some way away from his boat. I gybed over to him and he initially agreed to let me take him on board, but quickly changed his mind as another clap of thunder overhead persuaded him to stay in the water.

"He went ashore in the rescue boat to be treated by ambulance officers and spent the night in hospital.

"The hull was a write-off. The deck had lifted off from the bow to the cockpit. There were two holes in the hull below the waterline one third down from the bow. There was a huge hole at the gunwale opposite the mast.

"The mast step had separated from the hull. The rivets on the mast had melted and the top section had dropped into the bottom section. The lightning exited through the top of the sail sock."

The someone who had to say it was Zac Skulander, another competitor: "Chris was on fire out there today!"

Hobart's moving target

A SIMPLE QUESTION from ocean racing veteran and trivia aficionado Frank Sticovich about the course distance of the Sydney-Hobart race (alias the Rolex Sydney-Hobart race), set off a spirited and typically inconclusive email exchange with other aficionados, often to be found tucked away in a corner of the Coasters Retreat bar of the Cruising Yacht Club of Australia.

Sticovich kicked it off with a query to Tony Cable, the famed founder of the Quiet Little Drink and expert leeward runner handler on the maxi Sovereign and others.

"In the old days, the Hobart race was generally considered to be a 650-mile race. In recent years all the media seem to refer to the race as a 630-mile stint. Reading the CYCA's weekly news service this morning, I note that the race is now 628 miles long. I ask you, is the earth shrinking or something?"

Cable put Frank's message out to his usual circle of internet thumb twiddlers for some interesting responses.

From John Brooks: "The problem is due to a relatively unknown – to the general public – phenomenon of orbital mechanics. As any of us old navigators would be able to tell you, the present configuration of the solar system is such that the heavy planets – Jupiter, Saturn, etc – are positioned in their orbits on the northern side of the earth's equatorial plane while the lighter planets – Neptune, Uranus, etc – are positioned on the southern side.

"This has a tidal effect on the planet, drawing the earth's mass towards the northern hemisphere, making the southern hemisphere slightly smaller, hence the shorter distance from Sydney to Hobart.

"This also makes it clear the reason for recent record times. Some years from now, the phenomenon will reverse and the distance to Hobart will increase back to where it was in the 1960s, for instance and once again it will take even the fast boats a week to get to Hobart.

"To all those posing as modern navigators, you can't get that sort of information from a GPS, let me tell you."

Graham (Frizzle) Freeman: "Glark, I guess we now know why so many navigators have gone past the Dutchman (he means Tasman Island, I guess) before asking the helmsman of the watch to turn the vessel to starboard.

Navigators obviously observed the course distance as printed in the sailing instructions and deduced the distance from the Dutchman to the finishing line, which gave them the distance from Sydney Harbour to the starboard turn point at the Dutchman.

"Holler (as in 'Holler for a Marshall', navigator instructor Gordon Marshall) in all his nav classes would have made sure that his students understood this fundamental calculation of how to determine the turn point. It is a shame that the race distance could have been so incorrectly calculated and printed.

"Blokes like Magnus, Sighty, Stan, Bowker, Eppy, Bill, must have all reached the Dutchman during daylight; how else would they know where to turn? Bowker always made breakfast approaching the Dutchman and could pick the turning point by the hardness of the butter. He knew!

"Just imagine if the error was the other way? They would be shipwrecked on Green Island (on the east coast of Tasmania) without a pub."

David Fuller: "Being a one-Hobart veteran, I can attest to the fact that it is 6500 miles and I never again reprimanded my kids for asking, "Are we there yet?"

Garry Linacre: "I may help with information relevant to your recent raft of correspondence. As I have recently joined the marine navigation and cartography industry I am becoming versed in this topic.

"On every marine chart supplied or licensed by the Australian Hydrographic Office, Tasman Island is in the wrong place. If you navigate between Tasman and Tasmania, your GPS will show you have travelled across dirt. This occurs because Matt Flinders was pissed the night he surveyed the area and the Australian Navy, being non-existent or busy since the late 1700s, failed to update Matthew's information. The truth is no-one knows where

Tasmania or Tasman Island really are."

Tony (Glark) Cable: "If you ask the race publicists, the distance is irrelevant. It is only what a MAXI has to travel in one day to beat the race record.

"For mine, I do not know how long the bloody race is, they just make me do it. I will tell you one thing, though. Tasman Island used to be 650 miles, now it is 628 miles. In the years I have been going down, the dirt just gets blown off the top of it. I don't know how the lighthouse keeps standing there.

"In '63 going around, we had six inches of mud from the island on the foredeck. The for'ard hand had to be issued with a shovel before each sail change."

Ross Cable (also a Hobart racer): "Dad, being a big maxi yacht sailor from way back, you should have worked it out; the maxis are getting bigger and bigger, so much so that the last bloke who actually decided to measure it with his 'bloody new fangled GPS' was standing on the bow of the yacht (at Tasman) and the stern of the yacht at the finish (or did I get that the wrong way around?), hence the 3nm discrepancy."

Bob Cranse: To head off implications in other correspondence that the discrepancies were caused by the media lazily rounding off the decimals of the nautical miles, let's return to the absolute words in the official race documents:

Notice of Race for 2003: "The race is a 627 nautical mile (approx) passage race.
Sailing Instructions 2003: "Length of course: approx. 628.3 nautical miles.
Notice of Race 2004: "The race is a 628 nautical mile passage race."

All washed up
SAYING FROM HUGHIE Treharne: "She's so ugly, even the tide wouldn't take her out."

What it costs
THE SUBJECT OF the conversation, while we were milling around waiting for a start, turned to impecunious yacht owners – or rather those who pretended to be impecunious (don't reach for the dictionary, "having little or no money".)

Remembered was one owner who continually emphasised the need for care with the equipment by being able to nominate the price of every item on board. "That whip aerial cost $47.50, do not hold onto it."

One hairy night on an offshore race, someone did grab the aerial as the boat lurched and off it snapped. The crew on deck made a swift but meticulous repair with Superglue while the owner snored below on the off watch.

As he emerged on deck next morning and took a look around the boat lurched, he fell against the whip aerial and snapped. "I only just touched it and it broke!" he cried.

Same boat, the dish of washing up water was passed on deck with the instructions, "get rid of this". Over the side went the contents, including all the knives and forks, lurking unseen in the murky water.

The race was completed with just one fork.

Mickleborough turns 80

THE FUN-LOVING VETERAN Sydney offshore sailor Don Mickleborough as he turned 80 in September 2004, turned over some memories:

The 1963 Sydney-Hobart race was an extremely rough one for the tail-enders. Among the retirements was John Farren-Price's Lolita, dismasted and blown wide of the Tasmanian coast by a sou'-wester that topped 60 knots.

She was eventually towed in by the Royal Navy submarine Trump, which was on an Australian visit. Coincidentally, the navigator of Trump, Tony someone (Mickleborough is still trying to remember his name) had elected to take leave and race on Southerly.

"He was very artistic, he loved Turner's work," recalls Mickleborough. "It was so rough; it took us a day and a-half to tack into Tasman Island. Tony had given up trying to sleep in the forecastle, which we used to call 'Heroes' Headquarters' – it was such a rough ride up there – and had retired to a quarter berth. Then we took about 20 gallons of water into the quarter berth from a wave. Whereupon Tony said, I am re-naming this berth 'A study in aqua'.

Tony's naval experience came in handy later. "We were hard on the wind, under storm jib with the mainsail rolled down to about six feet, trying to lay Tasman, when a ship came around the corner, right on our track," recalled Mickleborough.

"Have you an "Aldis lamp?" asked Tony.

Mickleborough was able to produce one and Tony flashed a signal to the ship. Suddenly, bells started ringing, lights flashed and the ship altered course.

"What did you signal?" asked Mickleborough.

"You are standing into danger," said Tony.

It took Southerly 12 hours to beat the 11 miles from Tasman Island to Cape Raoul, with the winds between 60 and 85 knots in Storm Bay. At that time, came the folkloric quote from Doug Lintern, who had asked the young Phil ("Yogi Bear") Musgrave if he was scared.

"Yeah I am," said Yogi.

"Don't worry," said Doug. "We will be alright if we get out of this one."

Don finds a shoulder, Hobart 1978

The Fang Factor

THE SUDDEN PASSING of David ('Fang') Kilponen in Florida, at the age of 64 (in 2004) shocked and saddened the international sailing community.

Fang, who grew up in Sydney and raced offshore with Geoff Lee on Taurus and Peter Kurts on Love & War through the 1970s, boarded Jim Kilroy's Kialoa after the 1975 Hobart race and headed for a new life in the USA.

There, he carved a career as a yacht broker, built a reputation as a navigator and later – to everyone's s surprise – as a respected racing rules expert and eventually, International Sailing Federation judge.

But it was Fang's ability to tell a joke, captivate a whole crowd at a party and lighten up any potentially grim situation with a prank that we will all remember.

Untypically, he left us quickly and with nothing to say. Fang became seriously ill with pancreatic cancer, was admitted quickly to Fort Lauderdale hospital, Florida, where he suffered a cardiac arrest.

Neil Harvey, who was with Fang's daughter Paige from Sydney, Mike and Linn Sharpe, John and Loulou Boulton and Bob Fisher were at Fang's bedside when a doctor took him off life support, wrote in an e-mail to Fang's friends:

"We watched him slip away ten minutes after the removal of the medical equipment. He was at peace and for once, didn't regale us with his opinion, finally!"

Bob Fisher, recalling Fang's time on the maxis, recorded that he navigated others as well as Kilroy's Kialoas, including Il Moro di Venezia and Longobarda:

"Fang had a fund of stories, many of which he told at meetings of AusCrew in England and Quiet Little Drinks in Hobart and other places in the world.

"Often they were told on the weather rail to raise morale. But everyone who knew David Kilponen would know they were subject to the 'Fang factor'; he did have a way of embellishing his tales."

Peter Shipway, recalling the Fang Factor: "No disrespect, but Fang made bullshit an art form."

He remembers when he and Fang were mast men on the then brand new S&S 47 Love & War in 1973. They were preparing for a hoist in a race from Sydney when the spinnaker pole dislodged from its attachment point on the mast and crashed down on Fang's head.

He was carried below and put in a bunk, apparently too injured to continue racing but not injured badly enough to be taken ashore. However, as soon as the yacht returned to the dock at the Cruising Yacht Club of Australia, Fang, his head heavily bandaged, suddenly recovered, was the first one ashore and first into the bar to tell everyone within earshot of the incredible injury he had sustained during the race. Copious quantities of alcohol helped ease the 'pain'.

Harold Cudmore remembers Fang's wicked sense of humour. "We were racing on Kialoa IV, Jim Kilroy helming, myself as tactician, Fang as navigator in the world maxi championship in Sardinia. We all used to get a bit hot and revved up."

"One particular day it was Jim's turn to get revved up and we were all getting a bit anxious about it. So at one stage Fang gave me the nod. Jim asked me to spell him at the wheel. Fang slipped down below and the next moment, instead of sailing 9.4-9.6 knots upwind, we were doing 10.2, 10.1."

"Everyone's looking on, no-one's saying anything and the boat is cruising along beautifully. Jim says after a while, "I'll take her now," so Fang disappears below, we go back down to 9.5, 9.6."

Fang on jury duty

"And then after a while, for no particular reason, Jim says, "Will you take her again?" So I take her again, Fang disappears down below, alters the speedo for the second time, for 10.1s, 10.2s and at this stage Jim is getting very fraught because he couldn't believe someone else in the world could do this."

"He reckoned he had a handle on steering maxis and he did – he was a very good helmsman. So we had him completely wound up and we never let on. It was one of the few times in my life I saw Jim Kilroy a little bit subdued. Fang had a great sense of humour."

For his last 15 years or so, Kilponen moved from competitive sailing and devoted himself to the Racing Rules. He became US Sailing senior judge and ISAF international judge.

Peter Bowker, Fang's long-time friend and Friday night drinking companion at Chuck's Steakhouse in Fort Lauderdale, says: "He served as the rules adviser to the Italian America's Cup challenge in San Diego in 1992 and was largely responsible for the demise of the Kiwi challenge over the bowsprit protest (at least, that's what he told me so you might have to apply the Fang Factor)."

"Subsequently he navigated Passage (ex Windward Passage II) to win the Fastnet for Raoul Gardini after another rules hassle over her rating. Fang was somehow successful in navigating five Antigua Sailing Week overall winners, thereby winning five Rolex watches."

"In all, Fang was a great shipmate, raconteur and convivial companion. His passing is a great loss to the yachting community."

Remember Bill Northam

BILL SOLOMONS AND Mick York in 2004 restored Barranjoey, the 5.5 metre that Bill Northam, crewed by Dick Sargeant and Peter ("Pod") O'Donnell sailed to win Australia's first gold medal in sailing at the 1964 Tokyo Olympics.

Solomons chartered Barranjoey from Northam to sail in the 1968 Olympics. York, who campaigned with Solomons and Scott Kaufman aboard Barranjoey in the 1968 Olympic trials, could not compete in the Mexico Games because of work commitments. Sir James Hardy sailed in his place.

Solomons and York restored Barranjoey to sail in the 5.5 metre Gold Cup and world championship in December 2004/January 2005 on Sydney Harbour.

Solomons chartered her from the Sydney Maritime Museum, which had owned the yacht for the previous decade. The Museum replaced the deck and renovated the mahogany hull. Solomons and York fitted her out with new deck hardware, rig and sails. After the regattas they returned her to the Sydney Maritime Museum.

On the revival of the boat, it's appropriate to revive some memories of the late Sir William ("Bill") Northam, who was one of Australia's great sailing characters.

The wisecracks and jokes just kept rolling out but his business and sailing opponents soon found that he had a shrewd mind and hunger for success behind the comic mask and grin full of teeth.

Although he did not begin to sail until he was in his late 40s, he brought to his sailing all the skills of management and psychology that had made him successful in business and in Sydney town hall politics where he became leader of the Civic Reform Group.

Bill Northam's binoculars were special

Northam was a master of needling the opposition. The gold medal chase at the Tokyo Olympics came down to the Australians and the USA crew, skippered by Don Macnamara sailing an almost identical Luders-designed boat to Barranjoey, with the only obvious difference two portholes in the side of the US boat.

When Northam asked about the portholes, Macnamara said: "You'll see. You are not going to know what I am doing but I'll be able to see what you're doing through these."

Northam replied: "You've got 'em in the wrong place Mac. You'd better put them in the bow if you want to follow what we're doing; they're no good on the side."

Northam recalled: "He never forgave me for that one. And going out to the starts, we'd get alongside and I'd sing Macnamara's Band and he'd get really mad. He's a really serious bloke.

"The two boys didn't go along with that and I said, 'It's alright boys, you just do the rope jerking and I'll show you how this thing can be worked'. And there's no doubt about it, Macnamara spent most of his time watching me instead of what he was doing."

One of my own memories of Bill was when he was a spectator aboard a US Coastguard destroyer watching the 1967 America's Cup races off Newport, Rhode Island.

The destroyer was the official spectator boat. The heavies on board included the Australia Prime Minister Sir Robert Menzies and his wife Dame Pattie.

US Coastguard vessels are dry ships. As the brilliant Sparkman & Stephens designed Intrepid drew further and further away from the badly outclassed Dame Pattie, Sir Robert looked as though he would rather be elsewhere, although his wife retained a polite interest in the race, with the beaten boat bearing her name.

Enter Northam with a pair of binoculars slung around his neck. He took Sir Robert aside, behind a lifeboat, for a better view of the race. They emerged a short time later with the Prime Minister most obviously in a more cheerful mood.

Later Northam invited me to try out his "special" binoculars. You couldn't see a thing through them, but you could unscrew the lenses. They made neat shot glasses for the whisky contained in the body of the instrument.

Crocodiles? No worries.

THE NOTE TO competitors in the Qantas 2005 Tasar world championship organising committee in Darwin needs no embellishment from me:

"I am pleased to announce that Territory Insurance Office have agreed to come on board as our last Gold Specific Support sponsor.

"The organising committee can now answer the frequently asked question, 'What about the crocodiles?' "Your family now has no need to worry as every competitor will be provided with a free Crocodile Attack insurance policy which, as long as you die within 30 days of the attack, will pay out $50,000 to your estate.

"It also provides a very attractive laminated memento of their visit to The Territory."

True seamanship

I heard a piece of very good advice the other day about what to do on those occasions when practice sailing is cancelled for some reason but you are tempted to stay on at the club for a few long ones before facing the household chores.

You chuck your waterproofs under the showers, stuff them wet into your sailing bag and then ceremoniously hang them out to dry on the clothesline when you get home. Don't tell her I told you.

First Hobart race

The 60th Hobart race in 2004 evoked memories of the first. First-fleeter Ray Richmond fired the starting cannon while John Gordon from Winston Churchill and Geoff Ruggles from Peter Luke's Wayfarer crew were also honoured guests of the Cruising Yacht Club of Australia on start day.

Besides Rani, which after being listed as "missing" for four days emerged as winner of the first Sydney-Hobart race, Horizon featured in the headlines as "lost".

Aboard her was the then 23-year-old Alan Payne, later to establish himself as Australia's foremost designer of sound offshore yachts and of the outstanding America's Cup challengers Gretel and Gretel II.

Sydney newspapers on the "disaster" chase, interviewed Alan's parents who said they were not too concerned about Alan and the crew of Horizon, which also included 22-year-old Boy Messenger, another to make his mark in offshore racing.

Alan's younger brother Bill Payne hitched a ride aboard the Catalina that each day patrolled the race course to report on the progress of the yachts. Bill had been a pilot on the Halifaxes with RAF Bomber Command in England and also had good contacts in the RAAF.

"Geoff Nolan, an air force friend and I, were at a party at my parents' place when we heard on the radio that a Catalina was to search for Rani and Horizon.

"I rang Rathmines (RAAF base) and they told me if we could catch the midnight train to Gosford, they would take us along.

"I wasn't that concerned about Alan. It just seemed a good chance for a trip. The conditions by then were pretty calm. We flew around for a bit and checked most of the boats still at sea. We found Rani and that famous picture of her nearing the finish was taken from the Catalina. I think we found Horizon."

The Catalina landed on the Derwent and motored up to a mooring especially laid by the Navy, below Government House. A naval whaler dinghy rowed out to pick them up, endangering the Catalina's pontoons with its rowlocks.

They spent four days in Hobart, staying at the up-market Hadley's hotel, touring up Mount Wellington and down to the Huon Valley.

"We met Alan when he came ashore at Battery Point. He said, 'Good day' and seemed a bit surprised to see us. We also met up with Jack Earl and Bob Bull, who I knew, from Kathleen.

"It was a good, fun trip. We flew back with a crowd of 22 people on board including two WAAFs and a bag of lobsters. There were so many of us, Rathmines laid on another Catalina to fly us back to Rose Bay. Geoff Nolan and I just walked home."

Alan Payne also flew home after a swift-thinking initiative. Boy Messenger recalled that with flights out of Hobart fully-booked, Alan went to the post office and filed a telegram to his parents: "Send telegram, mother seriously ill."

The reply came: "Mother seriously ill, come home."

That was enough to get Alan on the first plane out while Boy had to catch the train to Launceston, the ferry Taroona across Bass Strait and the train from Melbourne to Sydney.

'So long' to Grimesy

ANOTHER OF AUSTRALIAN sailing's great characters, Roger Grimes, died in his sleep on the Gold Coast in 2005, aged 70. Although his health was obviously failing long before he passed away, he had his boat, the old Farr Half Tonner Hot Bubbles II, on the slips giving it a scrub and a coat of anti-fouling with the help of his son Richard.

Roger Grimes was a Sydney-based Qantas pilot who later in his many years with Qantas worked on its flight simulator program to qualify pilots at Qantas Base, Mascot.

In earlier sailing days he crewed aboard a 5.5 with Jack Carr and Jack Gale from Royal Prince Alfred Yacht Club in the 1968 Olympic trials. Through the 1970s he sailed with Peter Cole on the Half Tonner Bodega and became regular navigator on Jack Rooklyn's Apollo.

His overseas flying with Qantas allowed him to sail in the UK where he made many friends in British offshore racing. He crewed on the British yacht Synergy in the American Onion Patch series and Newport-Bermuda race.

He was a skilled, if sometimes unconventional, navigator. Tony Cable recalled that on one late call-up to navigate in a Montagu Island race, Grimesy made his calculations with a pencil stub on the back of a bus ticket and using a wobbly sail batten as a parallel ruler: "That's probably the nearest they can steer to a straight line anyway," he explained.

Grimesy was a wonderful seaman with a deep respect for the ocean. He sailed with us on the J24. "You always felt safe with Grimesy on board," my wife used to say.

Ashore his roguish nature, sense of humour and untiring pursuit of fair ladies could lead to complications. When he was sailing with us in a J24 world championship on Poole Bay in England, he enlivened proceedings in the welcoming party at the Parkstone Yacht Club by dancing on a table top with the commodore's daughter.

The commodore sent his wife over to tell the daughter to stop making a spectacle of herself. Such was Grimesy's charm, mother joined daughter and Grimesy on the table top.

One of Grimesy's last great offshore adventures was putting his hand up to sail in Michael Spies' crew aboard the tiny Triton 28 Tele-Rent in the 1992 Sydney-Hobart race.

At a wake for Grimesy in the CYCA, after a scattering of his ashes off Shark Island, Spiesy spoke about that race. They were short of crew: "We picked up a big Pommy bloke on the dock on Boxing Day," Spiesy told the gathering.

"I was reluctant to take him and said to Grimesy, "How do you know he is any good?"

Grimesy: "Did you see the brand of cigarettes he is smoking?"

Well it turned out that the Pommy bloke wasn't that good and was soon laid low with seasickness, down below, for most of the race. Meantime Grimesy smoked his way through the carton the pier-head jumper brought on board by Tasman Island.

And in place of the yellow waterproofs, clearly marked "DMR" on the back that Grimesy had bought on board, he ended the race wearing the Englishman's flash new Musto gear.

Tele-Net, despite the direst predictions, got to Hobart and in good enough shape to place third in division D. Grimesy delivered her back to Sydney single-handed.

Richard Grimes, another flier and a very good sailor inherited his father's roguish streak. At the wake, the junior Grimes straightened out a previously circulated anecdote.

The senior Grimes was delivering a large motor boat, with its owner, to Mackay. The junior Grimes, learning of this and on an exercise in the vicinity flying an RAAF F18 with a wing man, buzzed the motor boat seven times, with the two jet planes roaring overhead at 500 knots.

Roger Grimes realised straight away what was going on but the boat's owner, who was down below was panicked by the noise. "He came up on deck in his life jacket, dragging the life raft behind him and hollering 'Mayday' into a radio."

Foiling the fish

THE AUSTRALIAN MOTH class is considering broadening its Australian championship regatta to include a fishing category. This is in response to new angling opportunities made available by the latest foiling technology.

Chris Dey demonstrated the great potential of this technology when he won the inaugural Sunshine Moth Sailing and Fishing Classic with the haul of a hefty 3kg bream.

For those interested in the technical details, the bream was landed on very light tackle; in fact no tackle at all after engaging in a short but serious relationship with Chris's foiling rudder blade at 18 knots.

The technocrats at the Moth class are developing new scoring systems that combine racing results with landed fish weights (tagging is encouraged).

Anxious period

THE OWNER/SKIPPER HAPPENED to be on the mainsheet when the Wednesday racer suffered a massive knockdown in a big breeze. He fell onto the traveller and badly abraded his elbow. The blood was flowing freely and alarmingly.

"Get something to stop the blood", was the urgent call. An obliging girl backpacker on board for the day rummaged around down below and produced a large wad that effectively stopped the flow.

Closer inspection of the labelling revealed it to be a No Frills Maxi sanitary pad. His crew mates have since called the skipper every 28 days to ask him how he is feeling.

Whitehaven beach party

DAVID ("CHALKIE") HUTCHEN, one of the founders of Hamilton Island Race Week, at the 2006 running of the event was about to move from Airlie Beach, where he had lived for the previous 25 years further north, to Hinchinbrook Passage, told me how the Whitehaven Beach party first got off the sand.

Although that fun beach picnic eventually collapsed under the weight of its popularity, drawing hordes of backpackers and young resort staff as well as the yachties, it was a fun feature of the regatta for many years.

Chalkie told me how the first Whitehaven beach party got off to a flying start at the second Race Week in 1985.

"We put a semi-trailer full of grog

David Hutchen

The first Whitehaven Beach party, Hamilton Island Race Week, 1985

on the island's barge. As it headed off for Whitehaven Beach Keith Williams (owner of the Hamilton Island resort) asked where the barge was going."

Hutchen for the first time told Williams of the plan to drive the barge up onto the beach to supply the food and drink at a big party for the yachties.

Williams said, "You'll never get anybody over there."

"We will," said Chalkie. "We've let it be known that the first 50 cartons are free."

Chalkie told me the above while we were aboard his fast powerboat 389 (named after his favourite drop of red wine) on the way to the 2006 party. While we were relaxed over drinks, at anchor off the beach, the conversation turned to tee-shirt messages.

A much-travelled lady in the group, topped it with the tale of a tee-shirt she once bought in New York.

Its message proclaimed, "I am a virgin."

Underneath in small bracketed typeface: "And this is a very old tee-shirt."

Mr and Mrs Araldite

ROYAL YACHT CLUB of Victoria life member and one of Port Phillip's best-known offshore sailors Bernie Case, with his wife Lee, journeyed to Sydney to receive an award to recognise his achievement in sailing 40 Sydney-Hobart races at the Tony Cable-organised Quiet Little Drink cocktail party at the CYCA.

He has sailed in seven Admiral's Cups, seven Kenwood/Clipper Cup regatta and eight Fastnet races. He was in the crew of Bob Bell's Condor when she took line honours in the 1986 Hobart race and aboard David Forbes' and John Calvert's Great News when she won the 1989 Fastnet race on corrected time when she was under charter to Randy Short of the USA Admiral's Cup team and skippered by Tom Blackaller.

A crew mate from Case's early days in offshore racing, John Sheridan, in introducing him to the QLD gathering reminded us that Bernie was known as "Araldite" to his sailing mates for his reluctance to part with the helm.

Sheridan said that in those 1960s days, doing a Hobart race to Victorians meant a three- to four-week commitment also embracing the Queenscliff-Sydney race and then the Hobart before sailing back to Melbourne.

Mr and Mrs Araldite

He recalled that Bernie met and married Lee in 1966 at the Royal YC of Victoria in "a very happy union that produced six children".

"I was impressed at how Bernie organised the honeymoon," Sheridan said. "The first day he sat for his radio operator's ticket. The next few days we prepared his yacht Serifa and left in the Queenscliff to Sydney race and then the Hobart, getting sixth on corrected time; a great effort for a first-time skipper in his 32ft Jack Savage design.

"When you consider this start to the marriage and Bernie's long list of sailing exploits including 40 Hobarts, it's amazing that he and Lee are about to celebrate their 40th anniversary."

Sheridan introduced Lee and added: "She should get a Mrs Araldite award."

Technology embrace

HAVING TELEVISION AND film documentary camera men aboard Sydney-Hobart race boats, a reasonably recent development in promoting the big race, is sometimes under sufferance from the old hands on board.

One well-known forward hand expressed himself firmly when a strobe light dazzled him. "Launch that bloody thing overboard," he screamed. But later that night, faced with plaited halyards, he meekly asked, "Do you still have that strobe light? Shine it up here."

Purple spinnakers

ANYONE WHO HAS been responsible for blowing out a spinnaker knows the sense of great loss followed by the sheer terror of the thought: "How do I tell the missus?"

Some never do. I've heard of a boat owner who always had his spinnakers made of purple cloth so that his partner could not tell whether they were old or new.

Other owners strike special deals. At Hamilton Island Race Week one year that wonderful Queenslander Arthur Bloore blew out a brand new spinnaker, about $10,000 worth, at the start of a race.

His wife Fay, responding to condolences from other wives watching from the marina breakwater, just said: "Don't worry, it's time to take my Bankcard for a walk," and headed off to the resort's shops.

They're Irish

I WENT DOWN at Sturrock's in Rushcutters Bay to order another pair of Dubarry sailing shoes when the Sturrock brothers, Doug and John, told me that it was possible to order a new sole from the Irish sailing footware firm – a popular option with Sydney sailors because the hand-sewn leather uppers do not readily wear out.

I ordered a new pair anyway as old ones looked quite beaten up after being worn almost every day for two years.

In the process, the Sturrock's told me that Dubarry once sent them out a box of new footware containing two right-hand shoes.

The Sturrocks advised Dubarry by fax of the mistake and suggested they forward two left-hand shoes.

The reply: "We can't do that. We only supply them in pairs."

Sayings from Sayer

JON SAYER, THE Queensland-based yacht designer, showed a dry sense of humour in the wettest circumstances during the Melbourne-Osaka double-handed race in 2007.

Aboard one of his newest 12m designs with owner Murray Bucknall, in an e-mail to the race's press officer Di Pearson, he described a hard spinnaker run off the Queensland coast:

"It was blowing dogs off chains, decided to get the spinnaker down and rest; 18 knots of boat speed for six minutes straight.

"Very tired and weak from hard work, need bigger hatch area as Murray misses when throwing food out. Instrument covers work well (covered in food). Boat goes well.

"PS: Murray fell on my new glasses. The bleeding will stop soon – where I hit him with the winch handle!"

One size fits all

THE COMMERCIAL PROPERTY section of the Sydney Morning Herald weekend edition on November 24-25, 2007, reporting on various property industry players sailing in the Savills Short Ocean Racing Championship:

"One of those leading the charge will be Lang Walker, the head of Walker Corporation, racing in the extremely competitive Farr 40 keelboat class with his 52-metre luxury super yacht Kokomo.

Des Rodman brings 'The House' down

BROWSING THROUGH THE collection of photographic memorabilia on the walls of the Shipwrights' Arms after the 2007 Rolex Sydney-Hobart race I found a picture of the famous old timer Des Rodman with his dog and an accompanying legend about them both.

"Irish setter Cara is the only dog ever to have been centre stage at the Sydney Opera House.

"For many years the constant companion at sea of Des Rodman, former owner and master of the famous gaff-rigged schooner Flying Cloud, she was banned by security guards from an Opera House presentation to participants in the 1998 Tall Ships Race.

"Des wasn't having that. He said, 'We snuck away to another entrance and I came back with a pair of dark glasses and somebody holding my arm as though I was blind and she was my guide dog.

"It brought the house down. About 3000 people stood up and cheered!"

'Dive, dive!'

ROB MUNDLE, PROMOTIONS manager for Audi Hamilton Island Race Week,

Fidelis at Hamilton Island Race Week, 2006

revived fond memories from the finish of the 1966 Sydney-Hobart race in a press release about a classic yacht competition planned for this year's 25th anniversary regatta.

Nigel Stoke will be there with his beautifully-restored 44-year-old Fidelis, a 61ft sloop designed by Knud Reimers of Norway and built in New Zealand from triple-planked kauri.

Fun-loving Jim Davern and his crew from Auckland sailed the slender Fidelis across the Tasman and excelling in the light winds of that year took line honours in Sydney-Hobart race.

Mundle recalls that when one journalist in the dockside finishing scrum asked how such a long, lean and low-profile design handled rough weather offshore, Davern quipped, "Easy. We just sound the klaxon horn as we submerge and breathe through the mast."

Wise words

THERE WERE MANY great moments at the 2008 Yachting Awards during the Go for Gold Gala, a beautifully organised affair by Yachting Australia to farewell the Olympic and Paralympic teams.

Among the award winners were John Anderson who, with Dave Forbes, won the gold medal in the Star class at the 1972 Olympics. John won the Sport Professional Award 2008. He had served in the administration tirelessly since 1982 when he took on the role of development and technical officer for Yachting NSW.

He had also strongly supported youth development training and events.

On this latest trip to the podium, he concluded his modest acceptance remarks with advice to all aspiring sailors: "Remember. It's better to be looking down than looking up – or looking on."

Man of letters

DSQ DNF DNS PMS DNC DNC OCS/DSQ. Not too many regatta sailors could put together a scoreline like that but Ian ("Tinker") Bell, commodore of the Vaucluse Yacht Club, revealed the above as one of his when he was guest speaker at the Middle Harbour Amateur Sailing Club's annual presentation night in 2008.

Bell (who in the past era of risqué Laser names sailed a boat named Tongue My Bung), recalled his first regatta in Europe.

A new system dividing competitors into four separate divisions was being introduced along with a management system of tags, which competitors were required to collect from the regatta office before leaving the beach and return so that the organisers know everyone was safely home.

Bell returned to shore from racing on the first day to find himself listed on the results board as DSQ. He had forgotten to take his boat tag.

The following races did not produce any more joy. Soon his results included a DNF, a PMS (olden times language for OCS), a DNC (when he raced in the wrong fleet and ultimately the double whammy of an OCS/DSQ when he completely misjudged the final gate start and crashed into a bunch of other competitors.

"I ended up with no numbers, only letters, in my results and came 261st out of 261," Bell said. "Some of the other Australians pointed out that the American guys beat me and didn't even race in the regatta.

"Their results were just DNCs but because I had to carry two DSQs, I ended up with more points than them."

Tiller-Mate

KIRK WATSON, WHO was the mainsheet trimmer on David Pescud's Sailors with disAbilities in the 2008 Rolex Sydney-Hobart race, is visually impaired. He trims by feel; the breeze on his face, through the mainsheet he feels the pressure in the sail. Through the hull underneath he feels the loads and the motion of the boat through the waves.

Kirk Watson and Tiller

The headsail trimmers and helmsman help him. "Since I can't see, they give me a bit of a hand, letting me know what the boat speed is. We all work together; no different to any other boat really," he says.

He fits so well into his role that his crew mates sometimes forget that he has only minimal vision. Coming back from one training sail the helmsman said, "Can you take the wheel Kirk?"

Watson pointed to his guide dog Tiller in the cockpit and said," I don't think that's a good idea."

While they had to be parted for the duration of the Hobart race, Tiller was flown down to meet Watson, who did steer Sailors with disAbilities across the finishing line.

Chas faces arrest!

CHARLES (CHAS FROM Tas) Blundell, veteran international ocean racing professional and delivery skipper of yachts around Australia and throughout Asia, was apprehended by the police in Sydney in 2009.

Chas had only just completed a delivery voyage with a yacht to the Cruising Yacht Club of Australia in Rushcutters Bay and was walking up the hill for his two-monthly haircut in Kings Cross when it happened.

That particular morning the local cops were extremely edgy following the brutal bashing with a brick and robbery of an off-duty policewoman. Two of them on patrol, one and Asian female, stopped Chas who was in his usual casual sailing gear including the Drum reunion tracksuit top.

Where was he living? "Just got off a boat in Rushcutters Bay."

Where's your ID? His passport was on the boat. He did have two credit cards.

So they searched him. "What's this?" The small green bottle with the label worn off contained eye drops, not drugs.

What's this? The small jade figurine was a good luck charm. "You should know, being Asian," Chas volunteered cheekily to the female officer.

Where was he going? "To the Cross for a haircut. I always go there; it's only ten dollars."

Finally he produced a crumpled E-ticket for a flight from Sydney to Hong Kong the following day to pick up another yacht for delivery. That's when the coppers began calling him "Sir" and let him go on his way.

Pearly shells

DON MICKLEBOROUGH, AFTER an exhilarating sail on his Southerly in the CYCA's 2009 Great Veterans race, told me of a long past incident from the 1960s that had recently regurgitated, literally!

Southerly had been competing in an early race from Sydney to Port Hacking where the host club put on an evening of entertainment afterwards that included a performance by a comely young hula dancer.

One of Mickleborough's crew, a wild young teenager who would later become a respected yachting administrator, in a lucky draw won a few minutes alone with the dancer after her first show that afternoon.

In the course of that interlude on the club's verandah our hero, not wishing the young lady to leave him to appear in the scheduled second show, ate her shell bra.

On the return voyage to Sydney the young crewman complained of feeling crook. One of the old timers gave him a full bottle of Enos salts, which at the time seemed to fix him up.

But more than 40 years on in 2009 he began suffering acute stomach pains. An operation removed the shells, which he keeps in a jar at home and a helluva story.

Flying leap

CARL CRAFOORD CHOSE to meet feature writer Bob Ross to talk over his plans for Quantum Sailmakers Australasia at the Ship Inn, opposite the ferry wharves in Circular Quay, Sydney.

So inevitably the conversation got around to Carl's father Max, a notable offshore sailor of the 'sixties and 'seventies.

Carl recalled that in the days of six o'clock closing Max and a bunch of other sailors who were ferry commuters would gather after work in the "Shippies" and down five or six schooners before closing time.

That lent a new dimension to catching the ferry. One night, Sandy Schofield, panic-stricken that he was about to miss one, ran across the road and took a flying leap from the wharf onto the ferry – which turned out to be arriving.

Rolf rolls 'Salty'

Sadly and suddenly Rolf Mische, a fixture around the Cruising Yacht Club of Australia for many years as a sailor, fixer and philosopher, died in 2009. He joined the CYCA in 1954, crewed on many famous boats in everything from Hobart races to Wednesday afternoon scurries around the harbor.

He was a respected member of the University of NSW mechanical and manufacturing engineering faculty through which he introduced many newcomers to sailing as well as picking up handy ideas for his sailing, like a device to straighten bent stanchions without having to remove them from the boat.

German-born Rolf, who had lived in Australia for many years, retained a German accent and looked on history with humour, even World War Two. He used to point out its line honours aspect, "The Germans didn't lose the war. They were first to finish."

The story I liked best from Rolf's wake came from Jill Carter, who was sailing with him aboard Natelle when they were finishing a short offshore race in the harbor, neck and neck with Bill Psaltis' Meltemi.

Natelle had just hoisted a spinnaker when Rolf noticed that Meltemi's crew, in the process of hoisting a spinnaker, had yet to attach the halyard. So in his best Bill Psaltis voice, Rolf yelled: "Get that bloody spinnaker up."

The pit man dutifully went for the halyard and pulled it up the mast - without the spinnaker.

"Bill Psaltis came around later and said he considered it unsportsmanlike," said Jill. "Rolf just considered it to be smart sailing!"

Lion goosed

IN THE MELEE as the 2009 Rolex Sydney-Hobart fleet converged at mark X, first of the two clearance marks for boats leaving the harbour after the start, Bob Steel's Quest tangled with Lion New Zealand, the 78ft maxi that the late

Sir Peter Blake skippered to take line honours in the 1984 Sydney-Hobart as a shakedown before racing in the 1985-86 Whitbread around-the-world race. Sir Peter's daughter, Sarah-Jane Blake and other offspring of the 1984 crew were aboard Lion for this year's race.

Incredibly, Quest's bowsprit pole neatly plucked the port life ring off Lion NZ's pushpit without further major consequence. Quest's crew executed two penalty turns, retrieved the life ring and sailed on.

Quest wore the life ring as a trophy of the chase for a while from the bowsprit, when moored in Hobart's Kings Wharf Marina, before sailing master Mike Green took it around to Lion New Zealand with an apology:

"Only a cowardly Australian would attack you from the rear!"

Price about right

OVER DINNER ONE night in Port Lincoln, during the annual Lexus Lincoln Week regatta in 2010, Sir James Hardy dished up memories of former world 505 champion from Adelaide, Bryan Price, who died in 2009, aged 79.

Sir James told us a yarn about Price in the process of trying to sell his big sloop Sundowner after taking line honours with her in the 1974 Adelaide-Lincoln race.

Sundowner motored into the Town Wharf at Port Lincoln to take a prospective new owner on board for a race on Boston Bay. Two elderly ladies and a gentleman were waiting on the wharf with the prospective owner. They climbed on board and went below.

After a couple of tacks, a crewman went down to check on the elderly trio. He emerged and said, "There's spew everywhere". Farther along the course there was a crashing noise below. An investigating crewman reported that the elderly gent had a suspected broken arm.

Back at the wharf on disembarking, one of the ladies said, "We only bought two tickets and there were three of us. Should we buy another one?"

The elderly trio thought they were embarking on a regular around the bay tourist cruise. The prospective buyer said, "I've never seen them before in my life!"

Seen the piano?

THOUGHT I HAD heard all of the stories of outrageous post Sydney-Hobart race celebrations – Mickleborough romancing the department store dummy Delphine; Cable arrested in full flight at the Quiet Little Drink, etc – until a new one crossed the radar recently, courtesy of veteran navigator David Lawson.

It happened more than 20 years ago, but I have been able to verify it at the very source: a now respected Sydney professional man who for relaxation plays the piano quite well and fancies himself as a bit of a singer in the crooning mode.

So let's call him Perry Como. Perry, after crewing in a Sydney-Hobart race, embarked on a piano-playing marathon, which began in a popular Hobart waterfront pub.

One evening, after Perry had for some time been entertaining his crewmates and other patrons, he was asked to stop because the hotel's cleaner wanted to get behind the piano.

Perry's mates helpfully moved the piano into the street where Perry kept playing.

Then they moved it on, across the street and then progressively, with Perry still at the keyboard, to Constitution Dock. Eventually, as Perry puts it, "one thousand renditions of The House of the Rising Sun later", it somehow ended up on the deck of the yacht Perry had crewed.

Come morning, the owner arrived and awoke Perry, who had been sleeping below, with, "What's that thing doing on deck?"

The most expeditious solution for the furious owner was to undo the lifelines. The piano slid into Constitution Dock and disappeared. It's still there as far as anyone knows.

Another pigeon story

WILD OATS XI's rescue of a racing pigeon in the 2010 Audi Sydney-Gold Coast race evoked memories by Whitsundays sailor John Graham of a similar rescue on Port Phillip Bay many years ago.

The pigeon that landed on Wild Oats XI was a fortunate bird indeed. Blown out to sea by the fresh westerly breeze, after several attempts failed, managed to catch the flying 100-footer and landed on deck, exhausted.

Bowman Tim Wiseman later crushed fingers in a mainsheet turning block. When Wild Oats XI diverted to Newcastle to transfer Tim to hospital, navigator Adrienne Cahalan handed the homing pigeon in a lunchbox to Noakes Newcastle's Prue Harper aboard the RIB waiting outside the harbour.

Harper kept the pigeon at her house for the night and released it

John Graham, pigeon fancier

next morning. "It looked like it knew where it was going," she said.

John Graham's pigeon story happened on Breadfruit, a Bounty 35 owned by Rob Sill of Sandringham YC, during a winter series race in the 1970s.

The pigeons had started a race somewhere in Tasmania to various places on the mainland. Several days of strong northerlies had scattered them. "Apparently quite a few were never seen again," recalls Graham.

"During the pre-start in a 25-knot plus northerly, the pigeon crash landed in the cockpit. Noel Richmond recognised it as a racing pigeon (it had a tag on its leg) and hastily put it in the cockpit locker while we started.

"Once we were sailing, he took it out and as it didn't want to fly away, put it below, appropriately in a pigeon hole we had built to hold wine casks.

"It happily stayed there for the whole race. I think we forgot about it until we were back on the marina; no sign of it having been seasick.

"Noel wrote a short note, explaining why the pigeon was late, with his phone number and attached it to the bird's leg. He then took it outside and it flew away."

The grateful owner telephoned Noel the following week to say his bird had made the "Pigeon News" and became famous as the only pigeon to have done a yacht race in the middle of a pigeon race. "The pigeon's owner was apparently quite excited about it," Graham said.

Peculiar Hobart pranks

WITH YET ANOTHER Rolex Sydney-Hobart race not far away in 2010, yet another post-race prank has surfaced in dimming memories.

The Royal Navy destroyer HMS Glamorgan, on a courtesy visit to Australia, was berthed to a pier in Hobart outside the entrance to Constitution Dock in 1973. Two of the Sydney-Hobart race boats, Tony Fisher's ferro-cement 72-footer Helsal, which had just broken the race record and John Jarrett's 60ft steel cutter Banjo Patterson, from Melbourne, were tied up on the other side of the pier opposite Glamorgan.

Above Glamorgan's bridge was proudly displayed a plywood replica of the Welsh Griffin (red dragon) with the body of a lion and the wings of an eagle that features in the flag of Wales.

Over a few drinks in the cockpit of Banjo Patterson, Glamorgan's griffin became firstly a talking point and finally a desired trophy. Glamorgan had heavy security, but this was an open day with visitors welcomed.

John Sheridan, who these days sails with the Sydney Amateur SC, saw a way to secure the griffin. "I talked a couple of sheilas on the dock with near see-through blouses into walking up the gangplank with me," he said. "While the girls grabbed the attention of the sailors, I was able to slide away and get myself on top of the bridge to untie the griffin."

The crew on Banjo, meantime, had slipped their lines and motored her past Glamorgan to pick up the griffin as Sheridan threw it over the side.

Banjo was so close that her rigging hooked one of the security lights protruding from HMS Glamorgan. Unbelievably, it dropped neatly down the open forehatch of Banjo into the sail locker.

On returning to the wharf, Banjo's crew hoisted the griffin up her mast. "This infuriated the crew of HMS Glamorgan, particularly the Welsh sailors on board," says Sheridan. "They sent a war party down, with hacksaws, threatening to cut the mast down if they didn't get the griffin back."

Sheridan, meantime, had gone into hiding on Helsal. "Some officers from Glamorgan turned up at Banjo and told John Jarrett, 'You have got to give us this guy.

John Sheridan in trademark Sydney-Hobart headgear

On top of the bridge we've got some high-powered radio-active equipment and there's a good chance he has a dose of radiation', so they had to turn me over," says Sheridan.

"A couple of big naval police frog-marched me down to the ship."

He was taken to ship's infirmary, stripped, dressed in a hospital gown and placed in the de-contamination chamber. When Sheridan emerged, he was told the news was bad: "Your balls will be about as good for you now as a pair of pickled onions."

"They pulled out this big needle and scared the living daylights out of me, then began to laugh and I realised it was all a big joke."

Officers took him to the wardroom and over shared drinks told him, "We have to make this look good because the other ranks are most unhappy."

So agreement was reached. Banjo gave the griffin back. Glamorgan gave Banjo a souvenir red griffin plaque and a piece of timber from Nelson's flagship, HMS Victory. John Jarrett also gave Glamorgan the plaque from her cabin bulkhead inscribed with verses from "The man from Snowy River".

Banjo crew-member David ("Chalkie") Hutchen had that plaque made for Jarrett when the boat was launched. "He's still a bit peeved about losing it," says Sheridan.

Angry Cable

FAMOUS OCEAN RACER (45 Hobart races on the CV) Tony Cable embarked on a completely different offshore experience and technology tussle as a crew member of JBW, radio relay vessel in the 2011 Sydney-Southport race.

On watch in the bridge one night, a satnav 'phone began beeping urgently.

He picked it up and over what he described as "burble, burble, burble", he made out the words "anger management".

Believing he was on the receiving of a cold caller trying to sell him something in the way of psychological help, he snapped back, "I don't need any of that!" And hung up.

Crew mates, helpless with laughter, reminded him it was the name of a boat in the race.

Shifty's Odyssey

STEVE ("SHIFTY") OLD for countless years lived on New Beach Road right opposite the Cruising Yacht Club of Australia's Sydney clubhouse. He sailed, drove photo boats and became a fixture there.

In 2011 he relocated to the country but faithfully every Thursday catches the train for a journey of nearly three hours from Lithgow to Sydney to attend the CYCA's evening badge draw. It presents a good opportunity to catch up with old timers and maybe win the jackpot prize, which hovers up to and around $2000 before it goes off.

Following one such evening, he related: "My weekly train journey back to Lithgow, as you can imagine, is often long and boring, especially with a belly-full of beer.

"However last night there was a bit of comedy to relieve that boredom. The police (the real ones, not the transit blokes) came through the train checking tickets.

"It turned out the bloke in front of me didn't have a ticket and appeared to be miffed when asked to produce one and expressed his displeasure at the request.

"The copper asked him for some ID and he claimed, rather haughtily, to not have any; whereupon the copper politely informed that if he could not produce any ID he would be obliged to place him under arrest and escort him to the nearest police station.

"The bloke then nervously rustled through his bag and produced a letter as ID.

"The letter was an infringement notice - for fare evasion."

www.ingramcontent.com/pod-product-compliance
Lightning Source LLC
Chambersburg PA
CBHW070118110526
44587CB00014BA/2157